Winter Park

CHRONICLES

Winter Park
CHRONICLES

Gayle Prince Rajtar & Steve Rajtar

THE
History
PRESS

Published by The History Press
Charleston, SC   29403
www.historypress.net

Front Cover Images: Courtesy of the author and the Library of Congress's Historic American Landscape Survey Collection.

First published 2011

ISBN 9781540225061

Library of Congress Cataloging-in-Publication Data

Rajtar, Gayle Prince.
Winter Park chronicles / Gayle Prince Rajtar and Steve Rajtar.
p. cm.
Includes bibliographical references.
ISBN 9781540225061
1. Winter Park (Fla.)--History. 2. Winter Park (Fla.)--Social life and customs. 3. Winter
Park (Fla.)--Biography. 4. Rollins, Alonzo W., 1832-1887. 5. Rollins College (Winter Park,
Fla.)--History. 6. Historic buildings--Florida--Winter Park. 7. Historic sites--Florida--
Winter Park. I. Rajtar, Steve, 1951- II. Title.
F319.W79R34 2011
975.9'24--dc22
2011005031

CONTENTS

CONTENTS

INTRODUCTION

In 2008, an old friend named Jim Clark approached us and asked if we'd be interested in writing for a monthly magazine that he and others were organizing, which would be published by Knob Hill Media, LLC. He had read our book, *A Guide to Historic Winter Park, Florida*, and wanted us to contribute a Memories column focusing on a noteworthy person, place or event from the city's history. Of course, we said yes.

Since the first issue in December 2008, we've had great fun writing about the founding of the city, the early churches, Rollins College and more. We've also been fascinated with some of the more memorable people who have left their marks on Winter Park, including an unconventional college president, a movie star and a couple of professional baseball players who donned college uniforms. Some of the more recent subjects triggered fond memories for readers, such as the Winter Park Mall, the Langford Hotel and the huge sinkhole that brought national attention to the city.

Jim Clark, who is no longer with the magazine, first suggested a book featuring a collection of our Memories columns and was supported by current Knob Hill president Jim DeSimone. We appreciate the encouragement and camaraderie among all who have been or are still involved in creating such a beautiful magazine to represent an extraordinary city. We want to give special thanks to former editor Mick Lochridge, who was a joy to work with on these articles, and we wish him well in his future endeavors.

Thank you, Knob Hill, for consenting to the republication of these articles for this book. Thank you, Winter Park, for having so many interesting topics to write about.

The columns are printed essentially as they appeared in *Winter Park Magazine* (but often with different photos), with some new section headings and just a couple of substantive additions. After the magazine was published, former Rollins College president Thaddeus Seymour provided us with additional information about the 1985 Animated Magazine, and engineer Jim Jammal recounted the story of a driver whose car was rescued from the huge Winter Park sinkhole. Their contributions have been added to the original text. We've rearranged the articles in approximate chronological order, noting the date they originally appeared in the magazine.

The city of Winter Park was planned by its founders to be an extraordinary home for extraordinary people. It remains so today in many ways because of the people, places and events that are described in the following chapters.

Gayle Prince Rajtar
Steve Rajtar

Chapter 1

CITY FOR ALL SEASONS

Early Settlers Realize Their Dreams

Just north of Orlando, settlers built their homes in "one of the finest and most beautiful sections of the state…exactly in the heart of the peninsula," an article in the *New York Times* in February 1892 recalled about the early days of Winter Park. They enjoyed the mild climate and were content simply to live along the shores of beautiful lakes away from city life.

That all changed when men with a vision of the future arrived and catapulted their dream city into a real one.

A HOME WITH A VIEW

One of the earliest settlers was twenty-five-year-old David W. Mizell, who arrived in 1858 from Alachua County. He built a cabin on eight acres along the eastern shore of Lake Osceola for himself and his family. In addition to growing cotton, he raised horses, cattle, hogs, turkeys and goats. He named his homestead Lake View, but it was renamed Osceola in 1879 to honor a Seminole Indian chief.

Years later, Chicago businessman William C. Comstock arrived. Born in 1847 in Oswego, New York, he attended Northwestern University, where he earned bachelor's and master's degrees. He was involved in the grain business in Chicago and served as president of the Chicago Board of Trade for almost fifty years. He moved to this area as early as 1876 and later built his home, Eastbank.

But it was another Chicago businessman—Loring A. Chase—who saw more than just a nice place to build a home.

CLIMATE CHANGE

Born in New Hampshire in 1839, he was orphaned at the age of two and was raised in Canton, Massachusetts, by his aunt and uncle. After serving in the military in the Civil War, Chase moved to Chicago in 1864 and worked in several fields, including a stint as a real estate broker. After years of strenuous employment, his health declined, and in 1880, he was advised by his doctor to seek a warmer climate. Chase first visited Florida in February 1881 in search of good health, not real estate.

A tour of Orange County included the shores of Lakes Osceola and Virginia. "Never will the delightful impression of that first visit be obliterated from my mind," he recalled in a speech several years later.

He began to fantasize about building a town in the middle of that beautiful wilderness as a winter retreat for wealthy northerners. His dream gained momentum after a chance encounter with his boyhood friend, Oliver E. Chapman. Chapman's family was in the railroad business, and he was involved in wholesale imports.

PARTNERSHIP FORMED

Chase shared his hopes with the thirty-year-old Chapman, who enthusiastically supported his vision after they visited the area together in April 1881. Soon after, they bought about eight hundred acres, spending $13,000 on what would become the city of Winter Park.

Most historians consider Mizell, Comstock, Chase and Chapman the founders of the town. But there was another man—Wilson Phelps—who helped reassure Chase and Chapman that their dream could become a reality. Phelps owned land on Lake Osceola, where he built a home in 1875 and sold land to some of the early pioneers.

Chase and Chapman turned to Phelps for support in their efforts to create a residential community of winter homes for affluent northerners. He responded in a letter dated August 12, 1881. In it, Phelps extolled the virtues of the area, stating, "The climate is superb."

Let the Sun Shine

Phelps wrote that after his "experience of 54 years" in New York, Ohio and Illinois, he was "nearly dead with bronchitis of thirty years standing" until relocating to what he referred to as South Florida, which, at that time, meant any part of the state south of the Panhandle. Phelps raved about "the beneficial effects of this climate upon persons afflicted with consumption, catarrh, asthma and bronchitis" and "that a continued residence here has cured several of my acquaintances completely" and said he was himself cured.

His "honest advice to everybody afflicted with the above named problems, is to come to South Florida and be cured." Phelps offered to provide the names of other residents who would confirm his statements, including Comstock, his next-door neighbor.

He included the average temperatures for summers and winter, a description of the tropical breezes, the soil being well suited for growing citrus and the location as "below the frost line." The land was beautiful and, in his opinion, would continue to rise in value.

Phelps assured Chase and Chapman they had made a sound purchase and encouraged them to market it to their friends and "Northern men of means" with no hesitation. He essentially confirmed the wisdom of their purchase, and on August 29, 1881, Chase and Chapman officially named the community Winter Park and began advertising their new town in the Northeast.

On Track

A major contributing factor to Winter Park's development was the progress of the South Florida Railroad, which originally was incorporated by Edward W. Henck of Longwood in 1878. His tenacious efforts to overcome financial struggles and a battle for a state-issued charter and land grants led him to contact Royal M. Pulsifer, the principal owner of the *Boston Herald* and whose partner was the brother of one of the South Florida Railroad's founders. Pulsifer agreed to finance the completion of the railroad from Sanford to Orlando, which began running in November 1880 and proved to be the catalyst that sparked the development of Winter Park.

The railroad contributed greatly to Chase and Chapman's success, as did the development of local roads. Their detailed plans included parks, schools, hotels, a business district and a separate area for black residents.

The deliberate execution of those plans and successful, impassioned marketing resulted in an increase in the population, which grew from twelve families in 1881 to six hundred people by 1884, and Winter Park established itself as a city on the rise.

In Good Company

In 1885, Chase bought out Chapman's share of their partnership for $40,000 and formed the Winter Park Company with several prominent men whose names still can be seen along the streets of the city. They include Frederick Lyman, Franklin Fairbanks, F.G. Webster, Alonzo Rollins, William Comstock and J.F. Welbourne.

Today's residents of Winter Park should feel indebted to the city's founding fathers, but in particular to Chase, who translated his fantasy into a well-planned, extraordinary community. During the opening of a school several years after the founding of Winter Park, Chase told of his first visit as he viewed the pine forests and recalled: "The idea of a town of winter homes on this delightful spot took full possession of me."

This article first appeared in the December 2008 issue of Winter Park Magazine.

Chapter 2

INSPIRED BEGINNINGS

Churches Welcome Town's Early Worshippers

The history of the Congregational church in Winter Park is almost as old as the city itself. The house of worship was founded during "the formative [years] of Winter Park, was nurtured by the generosity, dedication and labors of the Founding Fathers and by many who then sojourned there during the winter season," according to Harry S. Douglass, author of *First Congregational Church of Winter Park, Florida: 1884–1984.*

In 1882, the town of Winter Park was barely a year old and beginning to flourish as more and more visitors decided to stay as full-time residents. Their need for a church was met by the Reverend Samuel B. Andrews, a Congregationalist minister from Massachusetts who invited visiting clergymen from a variety of denominations to lead a series of worship services. On October 8, 1882, Andrews officiated at the town's first religious service; it was held in the town hall above Ergood's General Store (at what is now the corner of Park Avenue and Morse Boulevard).

EVERYONE IS WELCOME

The Congregational church was well represented among the townspeople, many of whom came from New England, where the church thrived in the 1880s. The denomination encouraged new congregations, allowing them to be self-governing as well as inclusive, welcoming nonmembers to attend. In

The first sanctuary of the Congregational church was erected in 1884–1885 without the forty-foot steeple that was added two months after the building was dedicated. Its front door faced south, toward New England Avenue.

that warm and accepting climate, the Union Sunday School was established by twenty-seven residents—nearly the entire town—on December 17, 1882, and was led by a group of seven citizens of different denominations who established regular worship services. The Congregationalists were represented by Robert J.D. Larabee, a future deacon in the Congregational church who was superintendent of the Sunday school in 1883. During that time, enrollment in the school grew to sixty-four students, and the nondenominational services became known as the Union Church, from which developed the Congregational church and later the Episcopal and the Methodist churches.

Worship continued in the town hall and became quite crowded, especially during the winter months, as Winter Park's popularity grew as a destination for visitors escaping the cold North. One visitor, Dr. Edward Payson Hooker, was a Congregational minister from Lawrence, Massachusetts, who traveled to Winter Park in December 1883, despite his poor health, to oversee the creation of a second Congregational church in Orange County. The first had been organized by the Reverend Andrews in Mount Dora, which, at the time, was part of Orange County.

In the warm climate, Hooker grew strong and immediately began his mission. The first record of the church is dated January 24, 1884, documenting a gathering in the home of Oliver Chapman. Hooker presided over the meeting, and he, Larabee and Andrews were chosen to prepare a creed and bylaws to be presented at a meeting in the town hall a week later. Soon after, on February 17, 1884, the formal organization of the Congregational Church of Winter Park took place with twelve members.

Those charter members were not solely Congregationalists; the initial membership included Episcopalians, Methodists and Unitarians, several of whom had worshiped as part of the Union Church. Within two days, another meeting was held in the town hall to establish a Congregational Society, which was made up of the founding members and all who had contributed but were not actual members. The role of the society was to handle business affairs of the local church, including ownership of the property and the receiving and disbursing of funds. They worked with the congregation to adopt its Articles of Faith in accordance with Congregationalist principles.

SOUNDS LIKE A PLAN

A week later, the society had plans in place to build a sanctuary and had chosen a committee that included Hooker and local businessman Frederick W. Lyman to begin raising money. The land for the church was donated

The early worshipers in the Congregational church put up with uncomfortable benches and a lack of any source of heat other than each others' bodies. But, being the only church in town, it was still the most comfortable one.

by Chapman and Loring Chase on April 30 of the same year. The first sanctuary was built during 1884–1885 after the society selected a modified design from plans provided by the Congregational Union in New York City. It was located along New England Avenue, close to the northeast corner of the intersection with what was then Church Avenue and continuing to Welbourne Avenue, approximately where Knowles Avenue now runs. It was the first church building erected in Winter Park and started out with a flat-roofed belfry tower.

Dedication of the church took place in January 1885, and worshipers sat on planks set atop nail kegs in the unheated room. Lyman shrewdly commented in a letter written in 1914 to the church that this arrangement was "not conducive to slumber, and incidentally made…an uncomfortable strong appeal for more funds that proper seats might be provided, for we had adopted the motto, 'pay as you go.'"

ASK AND YE SHALL RECEIVE

According to an unidentified local newspaper of the time, "The Congregational Church here seems to be remarkably lucky in getting about what it asks for." Hooker preached a "practical sermon" titled "Systematic Christian Benevolence," and the congregation responded, especially Francis B. Knowles from Massachusetts. His generous donations and interest-free loans were directly responsible for the steeple and the parsonage.

In March 1885, a forty-foot steeple was added atop the belfry tower. It housed the 1,100-pound Founders' Bell that was paid for by Deacon Samuel H. Bassinger from Ohio, one of the twelve founding members. The bell was used to call parishioners to worship on the Congregational campus until 1940 when the first sanctuary was demolished. The bell also rang out to announce the decision to establish Rollins College.

Loans made by Knowles later that year helped complete the parsonage that was built on the west side of Interlachen Avenue between Fairbanks and Comstock Avenues. Thanks to Knowles and the tireless efforts of Lyman and other contributors, both the church and the parsonage were built largely debt free. The Winter Park church was said to be the only Congregational church in the state that received no financial assistance for its building or maintenance from the denomination's Home Missionary Fund.

A PERFECT LOCATION

Shortly after the church was dedicated, Winter Park was chosen by the Florida Congregational Association for the location of Rollins College. Hooker's eloquence on the need for the denomination's involvement in higher education made him the logical choice to head the new school. He led both the church and the college, and the parsonage doubled as the Rollins president's house. College classes were held at the church, starting with opening day on November 5, 1885, for about a month until they moved to the town hall location above Ergood's store.

As church membership grew, buildings were added. The Hooker Memorial House opened on May 26, 1907, and was used by the congregation as a social hall until 1940, when it was donated to the Ideal Women's Club and moved to Hannibal Square. It was replaced by the Hooker Memorial Hall in 1940, and the first sanctuary was demolished to

The present imposing façade opens on Interlachen Avenue. Inside are offices, classrooms, activity rooms and a sanctuary, which is considerably more comfortable than when it first opened in 1885.

make way for the new building, which was designed by noted Winter Park architect James Gamble Rogers II, who also designed the church office building in 1958.

SAVE THAT BELL

The Founders' Bell was removed from the tower and placed in the churchyard where it was hidden among shrubs and weeds. It remained there while its final resting place was debated for many years; it was finally donated to Rollins College in 1949. The congregation retained the right to approve the inscription on a plaque that would be displayed alongside the bell, as well as the location and the actual bell housing. It was placed in front of the Alumni House until 1956, when it was hoisted into its present location in the tower of the Knowles Memorial Chapel.

The bell that gathered early Congregationalists to worship on Sunday mornings and announced the selection of Winter Park as the home of Rollins College can still be heard today during Founders' Day celebrations, forever linking the Congregational church with the city's past, present and future.

This article first appeared in the October 2009 issue of Winter Park Magazine. *The photos of the former sanctuary appear courtesy of the First Congregational Church of Winter Park. The photo of today's sanctuary was taken by the authors.*

Chapter 3

BUILDING A STRONG FOUNDATION

Black Citizens Instrumental in Creation of City

Winter Park often is referred to as a well-planned city because its founders, Loring Chase and Oliver Chapman, were very thorough when they established and promoted their town in 1881. Among their ideas was a separate living area for black residents to support the town's growth. They couldn't have foreseen the impact one of those residents would have on the incorporation of the town that became the city of Winter Park.

CIVIL WAR'S AFTERMATH

After the Civil War, there were plenty of displaced African American citizens looking for a place to live and work in the South. Despite the abolition of slavery, land ownership rights were restricted, making it difficult for blacks to become financially independent. They had to search for places they could live and work.

Chase and Chapman were about to market their town to wealthy white northerners in 1881 as a winter resort and a sound financial investment for the developing citrus industry. Needing an abundant labor force to work in the hotels and groves, they welcomed the former slaves as members of the community. The west side of the town was set aside for African Americans and was named Hannibal Square in honor of General Hannibal, a Carthaginian military commander.

The Winter Park community had space for hotels, parks, schools, a business district and the two separate residential areas. In addition, Chase and Chapman had a receptive market in white northern Republicans, who were more progressive and receptive to the black population than southern Democrats. The white residents of Winter Park were comfortable with the labor force of black residents as long as, at the end of the day, they returned to their section of the town.

An 1884 map showed eighty-four residential lots in Hannibal Square designated as "Negro Lots" that were 50 feet square, considerably smaller than the 150- to 300-foot "Lake Front" and "Cottage" lots marketed to potential white customers.

No Man's Land

Hannibal Square had strong religious, family and community roots and developed its own churches and schools. Mary E. Brown and Mary McClure, former Northwestern University teachers, came to Winter Park in 1880 and,

Much of the social activity in early Hannibal Square revolved around the several churches located nearby. Shown here is the present sanctuary of the oldest one, Mount Moriah Missionary Baptist Church. It organized in 1886.

several years later, operated New Hope Cottage, a school for black children and adults. They held the school in their home, nicknamed "No Man's Land."

The first church in Hannibal Square was built in 1884 with the help of the white Congregational church. Surrounding residential lots were made available to "Negro families of good character who can be depended upon to work in the family or in the groves." In the following year, Methodist and Baptist missionary churches were built.

SELF-MADE MAN

Black businesses also were emerging. Gus C. Henderson, born in 1862 near Lake City, ran one of them. Henderson was a studious, determined young man who had lost his mother when he was just ten. He struggled to support himself, working for low wages while maintaining a strong desire for self-improvement. He tried farming but traded in his farming tools when he accepted a job as a traveling salesman for a New York company.

Gus Henderson not only helped the black residents of Winter Park but also brought relevant news and opinion to the black community of nearby Orlando. He died in 1917 and was buried in Orlando's Greenwood Cemetery.

He was successful, but after five months, the firm asked him to resign when a number of white salesmen complained to company officials about Henderson's race. Henderson, then twenty-one, was disheartened but felt that the firm treated him fairly by stating he was one of their best salesmen on the road.

Three years later, he found himself in Winter Park, a stable and accepting community. He settled there in 1886 and founded the South Florida Colored Printing & Publishing Co., becoming involved in the political scene.

Henderson, who was a staunch Republican with strong political views, stated in an 1888 speech in Hannibal Square that "all we ever received came from Republicans. Our citizenship, our freedom, our free schools, and numerous good laws that have done great good for the Negro came from the Republican party, and, gentlemen, if that party never does any more special good for me, I shall die a Republican."

Registered voters faced a challenge that year when it came time to vote to incorporate the town: they would not have had a quorum at their meeting without Henderson's help. He had been an enthusiastic supporter of Chase and Chapman's efforts to include black residents in their original plans for Winter Park, and he encouraged those citizens to remain supportive of the Winter Park Company's plans to incorporate. At that time, there were 297 black residents in Winter Park, of whom 64 were registered voters. There were 203 white residents, 47 of whom were registered voters.

VOTE OF CONFIDENCE

According to historian Fairolyn Livingston, "If it were not for Henderson's efforts, the incorporation of Winter Park would not have taken place on October 12, 1887, and Hannibal Square may not have originally been included within the city limits of Winter Park." Henderson violated curfew to lead a group of black registered voters to Ergood's Drugstore to attend that meeting, providing enough voters for a quorum, and the town of Winter Park—which included Hannibal Square—was officially established. Two black men, Walter B. Simpson and Frank R. Israel, were among the six aldermen elected in the first municipal election.

Henderson's charm and persuasiveness helped him secure enough credit to begin publishing a newspaper, the *Winter Park Advocate*, on May 31, 1889.

It was one of two black-owned newspapers in the state. It was the only newspaper in town, and it served both the black and the white communities while providing a forum for political debate. Henderson served as publisher, editor, reporter, advertising salesman and even typesetter for two years until he left the area. He later started the *Christian Recorder* and the *Florida Recorder* in Orlando and continued to champion black rights in education and politics.

SHIFTING BOUNDARIES

Politics continued to play a large role in the history of Winter Park when a group headed by William Comstock circulated a petition to remove Hannibal Square from the city in 1893. The black residents were mostly Republicans, the "Party of Lincoln." While there were more registered white voters than black voters in Winter Park, Hannibal Square represented a large Republican voting bloc. That worried white Democrats, who unsuccessfully tried to persuade the city commission to change the town limits to exclude the predominantly black Hannibal Square area. But they were able to persuade the Florida legislature to change the city boundary, despite opposition by the city commission.

Hannibal Square then remained outside the city limits until the 1920s. That's when city commissioners, seeking money for various projects, learned they could receive more state funding if Winter Park was designated a "city" instead of a "town." A city was defined as having three hundred or more registered voters, while a town had fewer than three hundred. Winter Park was short of that number, and its leaders wanted it to officially become the "City of Winter Park." They again needed Hannibal Square, and the boundaries were changed once more. Thanks to the black residents, Winter Park became an incorporated city in 1925.

This article first appeared in the February 2009 issue of Winter Park Magazine. *The photos were taken by the authors.*

Chapter 4

LUXURY HOTEL WAS A WELCOME ADDITION

The Seminole Attracts Wealthy Visitors

T he city's founding fathers intended Winter Park to be a resort destination for affluent families who wanted to escape harsh winters in the Midwest and Northeast. Fittingly, the new town's second building was a twenty-room hotel, the Rogers House, which opened on April 8, 1882. But for the wealthy to consider Winter Park an attractive destination, the town needed a larger luxury resort hotel—and the Seminole Hotel was conceived.

The Winter Park Company, founded by Frederick Lyman and other businessmen, considered a first-class hotel a priority for the young town's development. They arranged a $150,000 loan from Francis Knowles and laid the first brick for the hotel on March 26, 1885. The site was five acres separating Lakes Osceola and Virginia.

A VERY GRAND OPENING

The Seminole celebrated its grand opening on New Year's Day in 1886, with 2,000 visitors attending the festivities. At that time, the five-story hotel was the largest in the state. It could accommodate up to 400 guests in comfortable rooms that were equipped with luxuries of the day, such as steam heating and fireplaces, and suites came with private bathrooms and well-appointed kitchens. The hotel was managed by W.F. Paige, who also

Until it burned down in late 1902, the Seminole Hotel was the largest and fanciest place in Winter Park for visitors to stay. It had easy access to Lakes Osceola and Virginia, and aquatic activities were very popular.

was the proprietor of the nearly 1,100-guest Hotel Kaaterskill in New York's Catskill Mountains during the summer when the Seminole was closed.

A large portion of his Winter Park staff of porters, bellhops, cooks and maids were black residents who lived in Hannibal Square and who were neighbors of the servants of white families who lived on the east side of town. The hotel was one of the few major companies in the area that employed black residents.

The ground floor of the Seminole featured a long piazza, a covered porch running the length of the building that faced what was to become downtown Winter Park. An elegant one-hundred-foot-long dining room was on the same floor, which was referred to in hotel promotional materials as the "office floor," and its rooms were used for various purposes. Included were a large parlor, a separate smaller parlor reserved for use by women, a nurse's hall, a porter's room, a barber shop, a steam laundry, a reading room and the hotel office. The other four floors, accessible by both an elevator and stairways, housed guest rooms flanking a long north–south hallway and a much shorter east–west hallway above the lobby.

BEAUTIFUL HOTEL FOR A BEAUTIFUL TOWN

The beauty of this elegant resort was said to be matched by the beauty of Winter Park. At the north end of the first floor was a balcony with a wonderful view of Lake Osceola. The hotel brochure said guests on the promenade atop the mansard roof could see eleven lakes and that "the scene that greets the eye is one of surpassing loveliness. On every hand are the magnificent groves of pines, growing often to the water's edge, making a fringe of green around the lakes, sparkling in the sunlight. Thousands of orange trees are seen, with…their luscious fruit glistening in the sun like balls of gold."

Because the hotel was adjacent to two lakes that were connected to others by canals, water recreation was popular with guests. The Seminole was served by two steam-powered yachts: the *Alice*, which launched onto Lake Osceola on the north, and the *Fanny Knowles* (named for the daughter of Francis Knowles), which sailed on Lake Virginia to Rollins College and the Dinky Line railroad depot.

LOTS OF CHOICES

Hotel guests could listen to an orchestra, play tennis, croquet or billiards or use the bowling alley. Those who ventured from the immediate vicinity could enjoy great hunting and ocean beaches. Holidays were active times at the Seminole Hotel. For example, guests celebrated George Washington's birthday in 1890 with a slow mule race, a greased pig race and a climbing race up a greased pole over Lake Osceola. Some who wintered at the Seminole took a side excursion to Havana, Cuba, a popular tourist destination in the 1880s.

Access to the hotel was provided by the Seminole Horse Car, a mule-drawn trolley built in 1885 to accommodate visitors arriving in Winter Park by train. Guests could board a train in New York, and forty-four hours and 1,233 miles later, they would arrive at the station on the boulevard. The trolley would then take them and their luggage eastward along New England Avenue to the Seminole's door. Later, the trolley tracks extended to the Dinky Depot at the end of Ollie Avenue at Lake Virginia. The tracks were removed in 1903.

The Seminole Horse Car provided a slow but easy way to get from the resort to downtown Winter Park and the train station. From there, hotel visitors could travel to just about anywhere.

The Seminole attracted the rich and famous and claimed "that more millionaires and beauties were gathered on its piazzas than any other space in Florida." Several prominent politicians and other residents from the nation's capital visited the Seminole Hotel, including President Benjamin Harrison. President Grover Cleveland arrived on February 24, 1888, with private secretary Colonel Daniel Lamont and Secretary of War William C. Whitney and their wives. Local residents impressed the president and his entourage with an informal yet sumptuous reception. Hotel guest Jonathan Chace, a senator from Rhode Island, commented that "the Seminole is not surpassed by any hotel in the South."

A FIERY END

According to its brochure, "The Seminole has been made as perfect and complete in every department as money and skill could make it" and featured a "fire-alarm, and the most approved fire protection." Ironically, the Seminole Hotel burned to the ground on September 18, 1902. The fire began at 4:00 a.m. in the kitchen annex while the hotel was still closed for the summer. A caretaker was present, but he did not know how to use the fire hoses and was unable to extinguish the flames. As tourist season hadn't begun, there were few people around, and the only person who died in the fire was a man who entered the burning hotel in an attempt to rescue some of its furnishings.

The owners had insured the hotel for only $30,000, well below the original construction cost. They decided not to rebuild and instead sold the land for residential development. In 1906, the Reverend G.D. Simon Jr. bought the Seminole property, including the burned ruins. A cottage was built on a portion of the site by Mr. and Mrs. Harley B. Gibbs, and it was sold to Mr. and Mrs. W.D. Freeman in 1919. The property was inherited by Billie Freeman, wife of Rollins College faculty member and real estate salesman Raymond W. Greene, who served as Winter Park's mayor in 1953–1954.

Still known today as the Gibbs-Greene Cottage, it stands at 242 Chase Avenue on the site of the once-magnificent Seminole Hotel.

This article first appeared in the April 2009 issue of Winter Park Magazine. *The photos appear courtesy of the First Congregational Church of Winter Park.*

Chapter 5

SCHOOLED IN HOPE

Ivy League–Style Dreams Come True with Rollins

It isn't surprising the young town of Winter Park was chosen as the location of Rollins College, Florida's first four-year college. Progressive and farsighted northern men saw their community as a southern version of a New England town and wanted their children educated in the Ivy League style.

It's also not surprising that men from the Congregational church were instrumental in the development of Rollins College. Harvard, Yale and Dartmouth were all founded by members of the denomination. And, to no one's surprise, the growth of Winter Park echoed the growth of the cities of Cambridge, New Haven and Hanover, home to those Ivy League schools. What is surprising, however, is that it was a woman's dream and determination that led to the establishment of a college "for the education of the South in the South."

HIGH HOPES

Lucy Cross was an Oberlin graduate and former Wellesley faculty member who, at age forty-one, founded the Daytona Institute for Young Women in 1880 and served as its principal. She first envisioned an institution of higher learning in Central Florida while a member of the Congregational church and shared this vision with her pastor, the Reverend C.M. Bingham.

Lucy Cross deserves a major share of the credit for the establishment of a college in Florida in 1885. To honor her efforts, the Cross Hall dormitory was named in her honor in 1936, nine years after Cross's death. This photo is from 1910.

An announcement at the Congregationalist convention in Jacksonville on December 6, 1883, by the Reverend S.F. Gale deepened her resolve. "Hope sprang in my heart and an idea in my mind," she remarked when she heard that the first annual meeting of the Florida Congregational Association would be held in Winter Park in 1884.

Cross started work on a proposal to be presented at that meeting to create a local college and "felt there would be a response if I appealed to that noble body." Her paper was presented at the meeting on March 18 by Bingham, who said, "I do not dare to go home and face Miss Cross if I do not read this paper."

According to the minutes of that meeting, the response was to form a committee to "report on the Public School system of Florida, and higher education." The report would be given at the next annual meeting by Dr. Edward Payson Hooker, formerly of New England and the pastor of the newly formed Winter Park Congregational Church.

CHURCH SUPPORT

The idea of a local college was not entirely new to Hooker, thanks to Minneapolis business and civic leader Frederick W. Lyman, who retired to Winter Park in 1882. Lyman helped found their Congregational church and thought a Christian college would be an excellent addition to the area.

Hooker agreed, and based on that suggestion, on January 15, 1884, he delivered an eloquent sermon that was well received among the locals. That made him the perfect candidate to present the report at the second annual meeting of the Congregational Association, which was held January 28, 1885, in Orange City.

The association agreed it was time to take the first step toward founding an institution of higher education in Florida. The next day, association

The Reverend Hooker came to Winter Park to help organize a church, and he wound up not only as its pastor but also as the first president of the first four-year college in Florida. Poor health caused him to resign the presidency in 1892.

members recommended the formation of another committee "to receive propositions from various sections of the State in regard to inducements that can be offered for the location of this college," and the competition was underway for the first college in the state.

The committee included Hooker and Lyman from Winter Park, Bingham from Daytona, the Reverend S.F. Gale from Jacksonville and R.C. Tremain from Mount Dora. They reviewed proposals from those towns, as well as from Interlachen and Orange City, in preparation for the April meeting.

DUELING TOWNS

The competition was fierce, with each community claiming it would provide the best location for the future college. An article in the *Jacksonville Florida Times-Union* tried to convince local citizens of the benefits of the presence of a college. It also suggested that it was a bad idea "to locate colleges in out-of-the-way places, and in sparsely settled communities," which was intended as a swipe at Winter Park, which, at the time, had a population of 119 white families.

According to Lyman's account, Winter Park had the most intense campaign to gather support for the college, including house-to-house canvassing. Loyal residents felt there was no better location in the state.

The special session of the Congregational Association of Florida to consider the bids of the communities was held in Mount Dora on April 14. The Mount Dora bid included land for the campus, building materials, pledges and a microscope, valued at a total of $35,564. Daytona's bid included illustrated maps of the little-known city and $11,500 in cash. Daytona officials estimated the value of the Atlantic Ocean at $20,000. Jacksonville had $13,000 in cash and a choice of several locations for the college; Interlachen's bid was $12,500; and Orange City had $9,326 in cash, some lumber and land worth about $1,800.

THE WINNING BID

The Winter Park representative became increasingly elated during those proposals, as only he knew the extent of his offer. But he maintained his composure and even misled the gathering with a somber expression. His was the last bid, which included stock, land, and cash valued at $114,180, which elicited much despair from his competitors. Some claimed that the proposal was a dishonest one, and in an attempt to discredit the bid, they asserted that the land offered by Winter Park was underwater for a portion of the year. Association members decided to inspect the grounds themselves and to also visit Orange City before taking a vote.

The next day, the delegates arrived in Winter Park on mule wagons, riding through the city to tour the proposed campus site along the shores of Lake Virginia. This was followed by a ride on the South Florida Railroad to Sanford and a steamer to Blue Spring to view the Orange City property. But neither the Orange City property nor the cash could compete with the Winter Park offer, and its proposal was accepted.

The church bells rang out the news to the citizens of Winter Park, who gathered to celebrate with food, bonfires and a poem dedicated to Alonzo W. Rollins, who was responsible for their outstanding offer. Rollins was an industrialist who was born in Maine and moved to Chicago to start the A.W. Rollins and Co., but he had retired to Winter Park for health reasons. His $50,000 donation in cash and real estate secured the future of the college, which was named in his honor.

The original portion of the campus, built on land donated by Alonzo Rollins, was nicknamed "the Horseshoe" because of its shape. It retains its original shape, but the only building remaining from this early scene is the Pinehurst Hall dormitory, the building in the center.

SETTING THE BAR HIGH

Rollins College had high standards from the beginning because of the belief of the founders in "the New England idea of education, with the New England professor to elucidate it." A statement of unknown origin showed there were also high expectations for its success: "It is expected that Rollins College will be to the South what Yale and Harvard have been to the East, and that its fame as an institution of learning will rival theirs."

As one of the first American colleges to admit men and women, it is not surprising that the first person to earn a bachelor's degree in the state of Florida was a woman from Rollins College. That was a fitting tribute to Lucy Cross, "the Mother of Rollins College."

It had been her words that moved the men of the Congregational church to create Florida's first four-year college. "Vocally I cannot sing," Cross wrote, "but the song in my soul during the latter months of 1883 was a college in Florida."

This article first appeared in the January 2009 issue of Winter Park Magazine. *The photo of Lucy Cross appears courtesy of the Department of College Archives and Special Collections, Olin Library, Rollins College, Winter Park, Florida. The photos of Edward Hooker and the early campus appear courtesy of the First Congregational Church of Winter Park.*

Chapter 6

ALONZO W. ROLLINS

Man's Name, Legacy Changed Face of City

The history of Florida's first college and the city of Winter Park reflect their dependence upon each other. Rollins College could be considered the heart of the city, with life pulsating down Park Avenue and radiating outward through the rest of the city. The life-giving contribution that started the college came from its namesake, Alonzo Rollins.

Alonzo W. Rollins was born March 20, 1832, near Lebanon Center, Maine. He was one of seven children—five boys and two girls—and grew up working on a farm that had been owned by his family for two hundred years. Rollins never went to college, but in 1854 at the age of twenty-two, he began looking for new opportunities and wound up in Fort Dodge, Iowa, where he established a brickyard that summer.

HARDWORKING FAMILY MAN

He returned to Maine for the winter, but he went back to Fort Dodge the following year and persuaded his father, Richard, and one of his brothers, John, to assist him with his business endeavors, which included brick manufacturing and eventually running a paper mill. Richard Rollins went home after the summer season, but Alonzo and John stayed to cut trees and haul them to the Des Moines River, where they could be floated to mills after the spring thaw. He continued to influence his family, encouraging his father and two of his siblings, Henry and Sarah, to move to Des Moines in 1856. The two brothers and their father built a paper mill near the Raccoon River in Des Moines.

The mill failed in 1864, but Alonzo found success in his personal life the next year with his marriage in December to twenty-two-year-old Susan Ann Bowman from Royalton, Vermont. The couple moved to Chicago, where they were joined by Alonzo's brothers Henry and George. The textile industry beckoned, and Alonzo went to work for John Kinsey & Co., a dealer in cotton and wool goods. His expertise there led him and his brothers to form the mercantile firm of A.W. Rollins and Co., located on Michigan Avenue in downtown Chicago.

Unfortunately for the Rollins brothers, that location was ravaged by the Great Chicago Fire in 1871. Rebuilding began immediately throughout the city, and the Rollins company was no exception. The business, which sold dyes to wool mills, continued to grow, and their persistence paid off. Alonzo

In 1955, Rollins president Hugh F. McKean posed in front of this portrait of college benefactor and namesake Alonzo Rollins.

became a respected businessman and a leader in the industry. The company increased in value to nearly $100,000 by the mid-1870s, allowing him to accumulate enough money to live comfortably.

A DESIRE TO HELP OTHERS

In spite of all his success and hard work, Alonzo felt the money really was not his to keep. He was uncomfortable with his wealth, and his deep religious convictions made him want to help others. He was a man of high ideals and placed a great value on higher education despite never having attended college, and he often lamented having no children of his own to educate. A few years later, he would seize an opportunity to fulfill his high ideals that would have a profound effect on a great many children.

The harsh Chicago winters drove Alonzo and Susan south in search of a more healthful climate in the early 1880s, and they spent time in Palatka. During a visit to the developing town of Winter Park in 1883, they became enchanted by the scenic lakes and fragrant groves and decided immediately to buy land.

On February 1, 1884, Alonzo became one of the earliest winter visitors to buy property in the area, acquiring acreage along the shores of Lakes Osceola and Virginia for $10,000 from Alice M. St. Johns. Six weeks later, he bought an additional 120 acres from John and Elizabeth Scarlett for $2,500.

LOCATION, LOCATION, LOCATION

When Rollins heard in January 1885 that the Florida Congregational Association had decided to find a place in Florida to establish a private college, he knew exactly where the college should be located. He had once considered building a college in Chicago, but he had grown to love Winter Park and wanted to "perfect" the growing community. The lifelong Presbyterian decided to help secure the Congregational-sponsored school with a substantial gift: a portion of his Winter Park real estate, plus cash, stating that he had earned "every dollar of the $50,000" donation with his own hands.

Bids from several communities were presented to the state Congregational association, but with Rollins's generous contribution, the town's bid was more

This dormitory was named for its primary benefactor, Edward W. Rollins, a cousin of Alonzo Rollins. Embedded in the front wall just to the right of the doorway is a stone from the Newington, New Hampshire, homestead of their ancestor, James Rollins, who settled there in 1644.

than $114,000 and greatly exceeded all other offers. Winter Park was chosen as the site of the campus, and the town held a celebration, including the reading of an original poem by poet and editor Emily Huntington Miller, recognizing Rollins's gift. To thank him for his generosity, the school was named Rollins College.

On May 11, 1885, Alonzo and Susan Rollins deeded the land for the campus to college trustees Sullivan F. Gale, Edward P. Hooker and Frederick W. Lyman, and Florida's first four-year college was officially born. An announcement in the *Chicago Advance* newspaper that same day correctly predicted that classes would begin at the college in the fall. Even a thousand miles away, Rollins's influence on the Chicago business world was still felt.

YEARS OF GENEROSITY

His connection to the school didn't end with his initial gift. Rollins and his friend, Francis B. Knowles, worked together to construct Knowles Hall, the first building completed on the new campus. Knowles had also arrived in Winter Park in 1883 and never attended college. Both men wanted to share their personal successes with the community and hoped that future generations would benefit from their struggles. Alonzo continued to serve the school, holding the office of treasurer and then a trustee position.

His tenure in those positions did not last long. During a trip to Chicago, Rollins died September 2, 1887, but his generosity continued. In his will, he left forty acres of citrus groves along the eastern shore of Lake Osceola to the school. The groves provided income for the school until the Big Freeze of 1894–1895. The college then sold the land to Edward Hill Brewer. A portion of the remaining land owned by Rollins was deeded by Susan to Gale, Hooker and Lyman in 1891. Susan Rollins later lived in Chicago and Washington, D.C., and died on February 25, 1931, making a final gift of $222,475 to the college named for her husband.

Alonzo and Susan were gone, but their legacy changed the face of Winter Park forever. According to the Winter Park Company, formed in 1885 by several astute businessmen to plan the town, Alonzo Rollins was honored "as one of the friends and leading benefactors of Winter Park and Florida… His name is deservedly associated with all that Winter Park shall become and with the best interests of this Southern portion of our country."

This article first appeared in the September 2009 issue of Winter Park Magazine. *The photo of President McKean by the portrait of Alonzo Rollins appears courtesy of the Department of College Archives and Special Collections, Olin Library, Rollins College, Winter Park, Florida. The photo of Rollins Hall was taken by the authors.*

Chapter 7

DINKY LINE'S BIG IMPACT

Commuter Train Was a Boon to Students, Residents

Imagine being a Rollins College student in the 1890s and strolling through campus. You would expect to run into other students or come across a team on the practice field, but a train belching clouds of black smoke? Strangely, that was something long-ago students might also have seen.

The narrow-gauge tracks that ran through a section of campus carried a couple of bright orange engines belonging to the Orlando & Winter Park Railway. It was nicknamed "the Dinky Line" by students who commuted between the two towns. Here's how one described it: "That's just what it was. Even the rails…were dinky. Thought they'd never hold to the ground."

Before the Dinky Line, limited rail service was available to Winter Park from the South Florida Railroad along the developing area's western edge. Its passenger depot on Morse Boulevard was the first commercial building in the young town. The train made two trips a day between Orlando and Sanford, stopping in Winter Park. But in 1886, J. Harry Abbott saw a need for a more frequent, direct service between Winter Park and Orlando. As a result, the Orlando & Winter Park Railway incorporated on November 20 that year, with Abbott as superintendent and engineer and Francis B. Knowles as president.

With Lake Virginia in the background, this is a view of one of the two locomotives that pulled the passenger cars of the Dinky Line, which often derailed. Fortunately, they were light, and there were enough regular passengers who could lift them back onto the rails.

FILLING A NEED

To attract investors, Abbott developed a prospectus that cited the growing number of residents, tourists and Rollins students as potential passengers and noted there were "600 school children in Orlando with no educational institutions of a high grade, as yet established." In 1887, the Winter Park Company granted Abbott and his company the right-of-way to lay the tracks for the railroad, but he ran into problems with inefficient contractors and a yellow fever epidemic that shut down most travel and activity throughout the state.

The first train arrived in Winter Park from Orlando on January 2, 1889. The return trip was a scenic, peaceful journey—until its two coaches ran off the tracks. Fortunately, the train was traveling so slowly that there were no injuries.

The tracks ran from downtown Orlando toward Winter Park, passing through dense woods southwest of Lake Virginia and emerging onto what is now Lakeview Drive. The route then headed north between the lake and J.P. Morton's property, which later was developed as the College Quarter neighborhood.

A wooden depot with a two-story conical tower was built a little west of the foot of Ollie Avenue (where Dinky Dock Park is today). Its grand opening was held on February 13, 1889. That day, nearly two thousand tickets were sold, and passengers rode the train on three hundred short excursions. Reportedly, there were no delays or accidents, one of the few times that could ever be said.

REFINING THE LINE

Shortly after the depot opened, Abbott and Knowles sent a letter to the Rollins College trustees, asking them "to grant us the right to straighten our line, by permitting us to extend our straight line from the west of the campus, into, on upon the College property." Their request was approved, and a short section of the tracks was moved in March 1889, making the commute from Orlando more convenient for students whose families lived there.

Those who were using the South Florida Railroad had to walk quite a distance from its downtown depot, but now they could get on and off the Dinky Line on campus. The redesigned route also made more room for the soon-to-be-built Lyman Gymnasium. Francis Knowles died in May 1890, but he was honored by the naming of a Dinky Line locomotive that was christened the F.B. Knowles.

A SCENIC ROUTE

The tracks generally followed Lake Virginia's shoreline, going east on the lawn that is now adjacent to the south side of Elizabeth Hall and passing the French House before chugging through the front yards of the Recreation Hall and the boathouse and the backyards of Lyman Hall and the dining hall, called "the Beanery." The tracks then took a more northeasterly route away from the lakeshore, passing east of Rollins Hall and just a few feet from the Morse Gallery of Art's front door and on to the Ollie Avenue depot.

The tracks then continued eastward as the Osceola and Lake Jessup Railway, which incorporated on January 23, 1889. Its tracks hugged the shore of the southern half of Lake Mizell, running between the lakeshore and the dirt road later known as Genius Drive. It continued eastward to Oviedo's Lake Charm, an upscale neighborhood where residents had enough financial clout to get a station in their own backyard.

The two railroads combined on April 9, 1891, to form the East Florida and Atlantic Railroad, which in 1894 was merged into the Florida Central and Peninsular Railroad. In 1902, it became part of the Seaboard Air Line Railway System. Until 1903, one could ride the fragile Dinky Line to the depot near Ollie Avenue, switch to a horse-drawn railway that went up the hill and west on New England Avenue past the Seminole Hotel, to connect with the more substantial and reliable South Florida Railroad, which ran along the western edge of what is now Central Park.

AN IFFY TRACK RECORD

As the aptly named Dinky Line rounded the bends in the track, its locomotives and cars made creaking, screeching noises. It was infamous for its clamorous rumblings, snail-like pace, recurring tardiness and its "remarkable ability to leave the tracks" that traversed the sandy terrain, according to a description years later in the Rollins *Sandspur* student newspaper. Frequent stops were required to make repairs as students made the half-hour, six-mile trip from Orlando to Winter Park for fifteen cents, which included return fare. The Dinky Line made Rollins College one of the early commuter schools and certainly the first in Florida.

When the train broke down, passengers might walk the rest of the way to their destinations. But if the cars came off the tracks, the passengers would disembark and many would help the engineer lift the cars back onto the rails so the journey could continue. The Dinky Line also occasionally stopped to allow travelers to pick wildflowers or fruit. Sometimes the train was stopped by practical jokers who had applied soap or oil to the tracks. The locomotive would fail to get traction and an angry engineer would have to shovel sand onto the rails to get the train going again.

The passenger cars were yellow/orange, and the entire train was often referred to as the "Little Wiggle," with the two pitch pine-burning locomotives known as the "Tea Pot" and the "Coffee Pot." On busier days, the train made as many as eight round trips between Winter Park and Orlando. But the popularity of the automobile reduced the number of train passengers, and the Dinky Line was running only once a day by the 1960s. The Dinky Depot was torn down in 1967 and is memorialized by a small marker on the ground at the west end of the Dinky Dock city park.

END OF THE LINE

The last tracks of the Dinky Line were removed in 1969. A portion of its route is being developed as a multiuse recreational trail that will be known as the Dinky Line Trail. Those who travel this route in the future may not know that this path once lived up to its name.

This article first appeared in the March 2010 issue of Winter Park Magazine. *The photo of the train appears courtesy of the Department of College Archives and Special Collections, Olin Library, Rollins College, Winter Park, Florida.*

Chapter 8

THE GUILDS' DEEP ROOTS IN WINTER PARK

Family Plays Prominent Role in City's Growth

W inter Park's street signs, named for men of vision who founded and developed the town, read like a who's who of the city's history. However, the legacy of one man and his family can't be found on any signs but rather in the shade trees that line the city's roads.

William Augustus Guild was born in Dana, Massachusetts, on August 31, 1827, to a sixth-generation American family. He attended Harvard Medical School from 1849 to 1852 to become a doctor. But after finishing his studies, he instead became a pharmacist. He married Laura J. Barnes in 1849, and they had four daughters: Mary Latona, Laura Virginia, Alice Ellen and Clara Louise. After thirty years of dispensing medicines in Boston from a shop on the ground floor of the United States Hotel, William Guild decided to spend his winters with his family in Florida for his health.

A VISIT TO THE SUNSHINE STATE

Their first Florida visit was to Palatka and St. Augustine during the winter of 1880. The warm climate made a good impression, and upon the suggestion of friend George Frost, the Guilds traveled to Altamonte Springs in 1883 with plans to buy land there. However, after meeting Winter Park founders Oliver Chapman and Loring Chase and hearing their impassioned promotional pitch, Guild bought land along the north shore of Lake Osceola from Wilson

The large Guild family posed for this group portrait on the porch of their home overlooking Lake Osceola in 1884. A decade later, the adjacent citrus grove was destroyed by the Big Freeze, causing the family to abandon the home.

and Margaret Phelps. He cleared the land and set out a grove of orange trees. In the autumn of that year, his wife and daughters moved from Boston to their new permanent home in Winter Park.

Guild had the family's large two-story home built with lumber harvested from the Guild land and finished by Boston carpenters with cypress siding from a mill in Forest City, a community west of Altamonte Springs. The original paint and hardware were ordered from Boston, but they had to be shipped twice because the first order was lost when the steamer *City of Columbus* sank off the North Carolina coast. The home's exterior originally was covered with cypress siding brought by horse and wagon from Moyer's Forest City sawmill. In later years, the exterior was covered with stucco.

From the beginning, Laura Guild operated the family home as a boardinghouse for up to fifteen guests that was known by several names including the Osceola House, the Guild House and the Guild Hotel. Five of the sixteen rooms had fireplaces, and guests had a magnificent view of Lake Osceola from the wraparound porch.

ENDURING HARDSHIPS

The Guilds experienced other misfortunes in addition to replacing the original supplies. About six hundred young orange trees in the Guild grove had just begun to produce a substantial crop in 1886 when a severe frost ruined the fruit. The family was able to live on food from their vegetable garden until the area suffered a drought that hurt many of the local crops. That damage turned out to be minimal when compared with the Big Freeze of 1894–1895, which killed the citrus trees.

At some point, likely not long after the killing freeze, the Guilds are believed to have abandoned the house, and it fell into disrepair. It was bought by Frank and Maria Spooner in 1905, ending its use as a boardinghouse and turning it into a showplace. Maria gave it the name of "Weatogue," which has been thought to mean "wigwam place," "camping ground" or "here we camp." After the death of his wife, Frank Spooner sold the house in 1925 to Frank Matheson.

In spite of his bad luck, William Guild took an active interest in the young town of Winter Park and served as a town clerk and registration officer. He was instrumental in improving the town and teamed up with Miller A. Henkel to plant shade trees along the avenues of Winter Park. Guild personally provided and planted the trees along Palmer Avenue eastward from the canal bridge and on Park Avenue between Swope and Canton Avenues.

FAMILY PLAYS ACTIVE ROLE

The rest of the family also contributed to the community's development. Daughters Alice and Clara helped establish a reading circle in 1885, which evolved into the Circulating Library Association of Winter Park and today's public library. That same year, Rollins College opened with fifty-three students, and Clara Guild was one of the twenty-seven students from Winter Park. Her parents had intended to send her back to New England to be educated, but they were impressed by Rollins's potential to be as good as schools in Massachusetts. Clara enrolled in the "Classical course normal," majored in Latin and planned to become a teacher. At the time, the total tuition for the term was sixteen dollars per student. A receipt for another term shows the tuition was eighteen dollars.

Clara took five years to graduate with her bachelor of arts degree instead of the usual four. At the Girls High School in Boston, she hadn't received enough education in Greek, so she had to take additional courses at Rollins. In addition to Greek and Latin, her course work included English, mathematics, astronomy, geology, history, German, ethics, principles of teaching, education history, psychology, practice teaching, economics, logic and constitutional law.

ROLLINS'S FIRST GRADUATE

At the first Rollins graduation exercises for the Collegiate Department in 1890, held in the Congregational church, two students received degrees. Governor Francis P. Fleming delivered the commencement address to the student body, faculty and members of the community. Clara Guild is remembered as the first person to receive a college degree in the state of Florida because, alphabetically, her name came first. Ida May Missildine of South Carolina also received a degree that day and embarked upon her own teaching career, but she is rarely mentioned in any history books because she received her diploma moments after Clara was handed hers.

Rollins president and Congregational church pastor Edward P. Hooker described Clara Guild as "a lady of great excellence of character and life." In a letter he wrote in 1891, he predicted "she will be trusted and loved wherever she may be called to work and her influence will always be for the best things."

After graduation, Clara became an assistant to E. Emma Dart, a teacher at the Winter Park Public School. Her salary was forty dollars per month; Dart received sixty dollars. Clara taught at the school until 1895 and was its principal in 1895–1896. Clara spent the next three years as an instructor at the Grammar School Department at Rollins, and in 1898, she was granted her master of arts degree after completing her thesis, titled "The Child the Centre of Education." The school's first graduate then established the Rollins College Alumni Association and served as its first president until 1904.

Clara went on to teach and serve as principal at Sanford High School for thirteen years, followed by eleven years as a professor of Latin and history at the Cathedral School in Orlando in 1920. She was certified by the state to teach mathematics and English.

The Guild home, later known as Weatogue, still stands at 701 Via Bella. However, later modifications make it appear younger than its actual age of more than a century.

After spending a year teaching at South Carolina's Chicora College, Clara returned to Winter Park to teach high school in the area from 1934 until her retirement in 1939. She died a few years later in 1945.

SISTER ACT

Clara's older sister, Alice, graduated from the Massachusetts Normal Art School. After returning to Winter Park, she organized the Rollins Art Department and served as its chairwoman for a dozen years. In 1896, she joined the Winter Park Horticultural Association and was a founding member of the Winter Park Woman's Club in 1915.

Alice and Clara shared a house located at 419 Interlachen Avenue and remained in Winter Park after their father's death in 1902. William Guild's seedlings flourished, and the town reaped the benefits.

This article first appeared in the April 2010 issue of Winter Park Magazine. *The photo of the family appears courtesy of the Department of College Archives and Special Collections, Olin Library, Rollins College, Winter Park, Florida. The photo of the Guild home was taken by the authors.*

Chapter 9

PANSY'S PROSE BLOOMS IN WINTER PARK

For Author, Writing and Religion Were Intertwined

Inspired by the natural beauty of the area, artists and writers have long been drawn to Winter Park, and some became residents and developed international reputations. One of them was Isabella Macdonald Alden, an author known to most of her readers as Pansy.

Isabella Macdonald was born in 1841 in Rochester, New York, and was the youngest child of Isaac and Myra Macdonald. She was home-schooled by her father, who helped her develop her writing skills and gave her the "pet" name that she would use the rest of her life.

One day, while her mother was taking a nap, Isabella went outside and picked every pansy from their flower bed to decorate the dining table before guests arrived for tea. In her own words, she "picked the stem carefully from every one!…of course nobody would want ugly old stems laid on the pretty white tablecloth! Stems were to grow on so the pansy wouldn't get in the dirt." After her mother awoke, she scolded the child for picking the flowers, but her father took her side and gave her the nickname. She later wrote "my familiar name 'Pansy' dates from those stemless ones of the long ago."

Isabella Macdonald was a writer
and teacher whose life revolved
around her family and her religious
beliefs. Those concepts were
central to the stories she wrote.

PANSY'S CAREER BEGINS

Her first story, "Our Old Clock," was published in the local newspaper
when she was ten. To protect her identity, the author's name was given as
Pansy, and her career began. She was educated in New York at the Oneida
Seminary, the Seneca Collegiate Institute and the Young Ladies Institute.
She met her best friend, Theodosia Toll, while attending the seminary, and
if not for "Docia," her first book might not have been published. In 1865,
Pansy wrote *Helen Lester* for a writing contest but didn't believe it was good
enough to enter. She told her friend, "If I can't write a better story than that,
it proves I ought never to write at all. Tear the thing into bits and throw it
into the grate with the other rubbish."

Instead, Docia submitted it without her friend's knowledge. Pansy learned
about it when she won the fifty-dollar first prize. That was the first of more
than a hundred published books written by Pansy, who collaborated with
Docia on several books and stories.

MARRIED LIFE

Pansy taught at the Oneida Seminary where she met her future husband, the Reverend Gustavus Rossenberg Alden, and they were married in 1866. His work as a pastor took them to New York, Indiana, Ohio, Pennsylvania and the nation's capital. According to an article in the *Ladies' Home Journal* in 1892, "it would be difficult to find two people better suited to each other, more tenderly devoted, or more thoroughly one, in all their interests and aims…and it would be hard to imagine a cheerier, brighter home than theirs in Washington."

Pansy divided her time among writing, church activities, teaching and taking care of their son, Raymond, who was born in 1873. Her husband had a daughter from his first marriage, who, according to one source, lived with Docia Toll's family. Raymond's poor health led the family to spend time in Winter Park, and Raymond was enrolled as a student at Rollins College. The Reverend Alden served as a trustee of Rollins College during the tenure of President Edward P. Hooker. Raymond spent four years in the preparatory school and one year as a college freshman. After completing his studies at the University of Pennsylvania and Harvard, he moved to California to take a position as a professor at Stanford University.

While at Rollins, Raymond was considered to have great potential to follow in his mother's footsteps as a writer. He was described as "one of those men who succeed in whatever they undertake." He wrote under the pen name of Paranete and worked with his parents on the *Pansy*, a weekly children's periodical. He had a reputation as an authority on Shakespeare, Thoreau and Tennyson, prose literature from the 1700s and 1800s and drama history.

DUAL CALLINGS

For Pansy, writing and religion went hand in hand. Much of her literary effort went into Christian periodicals, including the *Herald* and *Presbyter* from about 1870 until 1900. She and her husband edited the *Pansy* from the mid-1870s to the mid-1890s. Children who joined the Pansy Society would receive the magazine by mail and read about missionary projects, news of new inventions and stories of Christian behavior. One of the popular serialized stories was "A Sevenfold Trouble," consisting of seven chapters, each written by a different individual with his or her own viewpoint. In addition to Pansy, chapter authors included the Reverend Alden, Marcia Macdonald Livingston (her sister who lived in Winter Park) and her son, Raymond.

Pansy created primary-grade lessons for Sunday schools that were published in the *Westminster Teacher* and edited the *Primary Quarterly*, both of which were produced by the Presbyterian Board of Publication. She also served on the staffs of *Christian Endeavor World* and *Trained Motherhood*. Pansy was an advocate for what she considered appropriate Christian behavior, and her books were essentially her interpretation of the Bible. Some of her books, including her most popular, *Esther Reid*, were partially based on her personal experiences. Her eight-volume *Chautauqua Girls* series promoted the Chautauqua movement of education and religion.

She often collaborated with her niece, Grace Livingston Hill, who considered Pansy as "a combination of fairy godmother, heroine, and saint." She described Pansy's writings as "stories out of real life that struck home and showed us to ourselves as God saw us; and sent us to our knees to talk with him."

Books Had Many Fans

Pansy's books were immensely popular during the last part of the nineteenth century, and by 1900 it was estimated that they were selling at a rate of 100,000 per year. They were translated into Japanese and French and could be found in the libraries of Sunday schools the world over. She had her own board game, titled "Divided Wisdom: A Game Based on Hymns and Bible Proverbs."

By that time, Pansy and her husband had their main home in Philadelphia, a summer home in Chautauqua, New York, and a winter home near Rollins College. In Winter Park, they lived in an imposing three-story "cottage" located at the northeast corner of Lyman and Interlachen Avenues, a site now occupied by the Residences, a condominium. The home had been built by her husband on land deeded to Pansy by the Winter Park Land Company in 1887. It had no plumbing, no electricity

In her later years, Pansy relied on her writing for much of the income for her and her invalid husband. After the death of her husband and son, she moved in with her daughter-in-law and continued to write until her death in 1930.

and a wood stove in the kitchen, typical for homes in Winter Park at the time. The Aldens sold it in 1918 to C.E. and Lottie Coffin, who two years later sold it to banker Michael McKenzy Smith.

SHIFTING FORTUNE

Meanwhile, Pansy had become the sole breadwinner of the family, as her husband had become an invalid. Gustavus and Raymond Alden both died in 1924, and Pansy moved in with her daughter-in-law in Palo Alto, California. Their former home was apparently lost in a foreclosure in 1930 and was then deeded to Luther A. and Irene B. Detwiler, who turned it into a rooming house known as the Interlachen Inn. It was sold in 1954 to Robert E. Langford of Chicago, the developer of the Langford Hotel and the Langford Apartments, who tore down the house in 1955 and, the following year, opened his hotel just to the north of the old Alden property.

Still writing at the age of eighty-eight, Pansy died on August 5, 1930, while working on her autobiography, *Memories of Yesterday*, which was completed by Grace Livingston Hill the following year. Pansy was buried in Cypress Lawn Memorial Park in Colma, California. Her works made a small comeback during the 1990s, and there is a website dedicated to preserving her memory. In *Cunning Workmen*, she wrote, "There is a good deal of time consumed in this world in planning for events that never occur. Sometimes I cannot help feeling that it would be an immense convenience, to say the least, if we could only know the end from the beginning."

This article first appeared in the June 2010 issue of Winter Park Magazine. *The first photo of Pansy appears courtesy of Daena M. Creel. The second photo of Pansy appears courtesy of Keepers of the Faith.*

Chapter 10

GEORGE MORGAN WARD

Financial Acumen, Loyalty Save Rollins

An "unsung hero" is a person who has shown bravery or has made a substantial contribution without being officially honored or recognized. That's a fitting description of George Morgan Ward, whose service to Rollins College spanned three different decades.

He was born in 1859 in Lowell, Massachusetts, to Sullivan and Mary Frances (Morgan) Ward and was a descendant of two famous Revolutionary War generals. In 1872, he joined the Kirk Street Congregational Church in Lowell, where he later was ordained as a minister.

A SCHOLAR BY NATURE

After high school, Ward entered Harvard in 1877 on a quest for education that continued for almost twenty years. He left after his sophomore year to work in Lowell, transferred to Dartmouth College and received his bachelor's degree in 1882 and his master's in 1884. He earned his law degree at Boston University and was admitted to the Massachusetts Bar in 1886.

Ward became involved with the United (renamed International) Society of Christian Endeavour in July 1885 and served as its first treasurer and then its general secretary, holding both positions while studying law. He resigned as treasurer when he began practicing in Lowell in 1886, but he continued as the general secretary and edited the society's official publication, the *Golden Rule*. Under his guidance, the Christian Endeavour movement was introduced into every state and territory, and Ward was recognized nationally as a powerful speaker.

RELIGIOUS CALLING

Poor health led to Ward's resignation in 1889 as the general secretary, and in 1890, he began a three-year stint in the mercantile business in Lowell, gradually resuming a more active role in the religious world. He entered Andover Theological Seminary in 1893, took additional postgraduate courses in theology at Johns Hopkins University in 1894 and became a Congregationalist minister that same year.

While Ward was studying theology, Winter Park residents were reeling from the effects of the devastating Big Freeze of 1894–1895. Freezing temperatures damaged Central Florida's citrus groves on December 27. January brought balmy weather and renewed hopes, and groves began to recover—until a second freeze on February 7 that brought even lower temperatures that destroyed both fruit and trees.

Rollins was greatly affected by the financial chaos, as many students went home, and groves owned by the college ceased to provide revenue. Rollins trustees had worked unsuccessfully since the school's opening to strengthen its finances, and they had spent several years trying to replace the first president, Dr. Edward Hooker, who retired in February 1892. They appointed Rollins professor John Ford as acting president and continued to search for a replacement. In October 1893, the college hired former science professor Charles Fairchild, a successful fundraiser for Oberlin College.

GRIM FORECAST

Fairchild was not living up to his reputation when the Big Freeze hit. According to the *Rollins College Bulletin*, the outlook was quite grim. "We have very little hope that there will be any orange trees left in the 'orange belt,'" wrote Mrs. Charles Fairchild. "If there had been a death in every family in the state we could not feel more depressed." President Fairchild abruptly resigned on March 18, 1895, and the trustees resumed the search for a financial savior.

Ford was asked to again serve as acting president. Salaries were cut, groves were sold and money was borrowed from a trustee. Rumors surfaced in May that the school would not open in the fall, but according to Rollins historian Dr. Jack Lane, Ford announced that "the trustees had voted unanimously to open as usual in October." The college did open, but enrollment dropped by 50 percent, and by December, the budget deficit doubled from the year before, to $20,000.

Ford did all he could to improve the situation, but his annual report in February 1896 painted a glum picture. He urged the executive committee to step up its efforts to find a permanent president.

George and Emma Ward were photographed out on a ride near the downtown Winter Park railroad station in 1897.

Candidate Ward

It was in this atmosphere that George Morgan Ward's name surfaced as a candidate. Ward was about to receive his divinity degree from Andover and be ordained in the Kirk Street Congregational Church in May 1896. His national reputation, impressive credentials and experience as a lawyer, businessman and minister brought him two job offers: the presidency of Washburn College in Kansas and the same position at Rollins.

The board invited Ward to visit the campus and then sent founding trustee Frederick Lyman to Boston to seal the deal. Ward accepted the offer on May 9, 1896, and assumed his duties as president and professor of economics and law on May 29. Soon after, on June 17, he married Emma Merriam Sprague, the daughter of a Congregationalist minister. Rollins College had its third president: an energetic thirty-seven-year-old with a magnetic personality and "flashing eyes" that an admirer said "could both burn an opponent and melt a friend."

Even though the trustees left out some details, Ward had no illusions about the circumstances he inherited. He later recalled, "They told me in the north that Rollins College did not owe any money. Well, I reckon it didn't. But the Trustees owed $5,000."

Ward made sweeping academic changes to revitalize the school and broaden its financial base by updating the classical curriculum. This attracted students to the prep school, but many were still lost to northeastern colleges. Ward wanted to increase the number of tuition-paying college students by appealing to a larger segment of the population.

Road to Recovery

The school began a slow recovery as the earnest president used his own money to make up the deficit. He spent hours revising the curriculum, leaving him little time to raise money. As he exhausted his personal funds during the first winter, Ward nearly reached the end of his rope: "I told the Almighty that if He was going to save this college He would have to do it Himself, that I was done. The next morning there was a pile of letters; as I opened the top one, out fell a check."

The $5,000 check was from Mrs. Francis Knowles, the widow of a charter trustee, reestablishing a relationship between the Knowles family and Rollins that would continue well into the future. The atmosphere at the school changed from "gloomy fear" to "confident hope," and in 1897, the college was able to fund its annual expenses and reduce its debt. The treasurer's next report was positive for the first time in several years, and by the end of Ward's administration, the college had a small surplus of funds.

FIRM FINANCIAL FOOTING

In 1900, Ward was approached by Henry Flagler, who offered him the pastorate of his Palm Beach Royal Poinciana Chapel. Once Flagler assured him that Rollins would benefit financially, Ward agreed to serve the chapel for three months each year. The arrangement continued for thirty years. Later, his Palm Beach secretary remembered Ward as forceful and direct. His sermons were "just a talk. Theologians…will phrase fantastic exclamations about the nature of repentance, for instance, but Dr. Ward would describe it thus: 'Be sorry for your sins but sorry enough to quit.' 'Be fit to live, and fit to live with' was another terse epigram of this sage."

Ward's absence began to affect the school's finances, and he resigned as president in February 1902. The reluctant board praised him, recognizing that he had "obliterated practically all the college's indebtedness" and attracted new donors who gave the school a solid financial base. Ward became a Rollins trustee in 1903 and resigned a year later to accept the presidency of Wells College in Aurora, New York, where he served until 1912. His successor at Rollins was Dr. William Blackman, who resigned in 1915 due to health issues. The board turned to Ward to fill the vacancy for one year (which turned into two without a salary), and once again, he used his financial prowess to get rid of debt and pay bills, leaving Rollins without a deficit for the first time in a decade when he left in June 1917.

Ward was not done with Rollins. He was elected chairman of the board of trustees in February 1918 during the presidency of Dr. Calvin French, who held the office during 1917–1919. French had grandiose ideas and presented a controversial financial plan to an astonished board in early 1919 with an ultimatum: accept it or he would resign. The plan was flatly rejected, and his resignation was accepted, and again Ward was tapped to be the acting president. He agreed (again without pay) but requested assistance, and James Brooks was hired as chancellor to spearhead an ambitious fundraising campaign, increasing the school's endowment by $503,000.

A LONG CAREER ENDS

In spite of this financial success, once again the college debt increased, and Ward felt he no longer had the energy to rescue the school. He resigned in 1922 and was elected president emeritus by the trustees. He came back in 1930 to give the annual convocation address during Founders' Week for Rollins's forty-fifth anniversary. Ten months later, he died in Palm Beach on the day he was to retire as the pastor of the Royal Poinciana Chapel.

Ward was more than a prolific fundraiser. He established the Latin American Program in 1896 that allowed Cuban students to attend Rollins. He updated the curriculum despite the protests of more traditional faculty members. His love for the school was best described in his own words: "If I could keep but one experience of my own life, I would keep the years at Winter Park. I learned there the real discipline of life."

This article first appeared in the November 2010 issue of Winter Park Magazine. *The photo of Reverend Ward appears courtesy of the Department of College Archives and Special Collections, Olin Library, Rollins College, Winter Park, Florida.*

Chapter 11

ROLLINS'S ROGUE "RUBE"

Pitcher, Catcher Ensure a Dominating Season

By 1903, baseball rivalry had grown fierce between Rollins College and Stetson University in DeLand. Each school set out that year to do whatever it took to claim bragging rights over the other. For Stetson, that meant recruiting top players from another school. Rollins, though, used more imagination: To guarantee victory, it enrolled a couple of Major League players: eccentric pitching sensation Rube Waddell and his catcher, Ossee Schreckengost.

Baseball fans, however, might not know that story. Rollins rarely mentions it in its records.

A SKILLED "HAYSEED"

George Edward Waddell was born in Bradford, Pennsylvania, in 1876. Little is known about Waddell's early years beyond his lack of a formal education and his propensity for erratic, eccentric behavior. Friends said he was "given to wild pranks and hijinks" in his youth.

By the time he was eighteen, he was a star on a minor-league baseball team in his home state and claimed his pitching skills came from his childhood hobby of "throwin' rocks at birds." Waddell earned a reputation as a good-natured, simple-minded hick and was first nicknamed "Hayseed," and later "Rube," the name that stayed with him the rest of his life.

Waddell began his professional career in the 1897 season with the National League Louisville Colonels and played for several minor- and Major League teams for the next sixteen years, most notably the Philadelphia Athletics from 1902 to 1907 during the peak of his career. He wore out his welcome with his childish behavior and his odd habits, but he was an outstanding baseball player. He led the American League in strikeouts for six consecutive years. His 349 strikeouts in 1904 set a record that stood for sixty-one years until it was broken by Sandy Koufax in 1965.

According to legendary manager and A's owner Connie Mack, "He had more stuff than any pitcher I ever saw." He described Waddell as "a big, loose, lanky fellow who was almost as fast as [Walter] Johnson, and his curve was even better than his speed." In 1955, Mack referred to Waddell as the greatest pitcher he had ever seen. Waddell was inducted into the Baseball Hall of Fame in 1946.

An Eccentric Hero

The Cultural Encyclopedia of Baseball History says Waddell was the greatest eccentric to ever play the game. He would skip games to go fishing or play marbles—or show up drunk. He might arrive sober but leave the mound during games to follow fire engines that went speeding past the ballpark. He usually changed into his uniform as he ran across the field, quite a sight because spectators claimed he didn't wear underwear. Sometimes he would go into the stands after pitching two innings to have a fan cut two inches off his shirtsleeve. He supposedly had a pet mockingbird that became so disruptive it was strangled by a teammate, and he once told a sportswriter that his real name was George Edward Harrison Reed Winchester Reuben Waddell.

Waddell also had a reputation for heroic deeds, rushing into burning buildings to help the local firefighters. Although reports were never verified, it was estimated that he saved as many as thirteen lives. One account reported in an issue of the *Philadelphia Daily News* in 1905 won him the local citizens' love.

Mack had his hands full trying to control Waddell, once paying him his $2,200 salary in single $1 bills, hoping the money would go further. He tried to curb the player's drinking and fighting by bandaging a man and staging a mock court proceeding with the judge (a friend of Mack's), threatening Waddell with jail if he drank again. It worked for one season.

PALS HIT IT OFF

The eccentric player's favorite catcher was Ossee Schreckengost, who also started his professional career with the Louisville Colonels in 1897. During the 1902 season, he joined the Philadelphia Athletics and was Waddell's teammate until 1907. Schreck, as he was known, was a catcher with a lifetime batting average of .271, good enough for the majors but not for the Hall of Fame. He caught balls behind the plate one-handed long before anyone else did. The Athletics kept him on the roster largely because he was the only catcher who could consistently catch Waddell's pitches.

The two shared adventures as well as a room and a bed when the team was on the road, which was common at that time. Fed up with Waddell's nighttime antics, Schreck refused to renew his contract unless the A's inserted a "no eating crackers in bed" clause in both of their contracts. Despite Waddell's protests, Mack agreed, and Schreck's contract was renewed.

The two players became involved with Rollins College while they were both professional athletes. Rollins played in its first intercollegiate sports competition, a baseball game against Stetson University, in 1890, which was the start of an intense rivalry. In 1903, both schools figured their best chance of winning was to bring in some "ringers" to dominate the other squad. Stetson acquired some players from the University of Illinois. Rollins figured it needed its own ringers despite having a future Major Leaguer, pitcher Del Mason.

WINNING STRATEGY

Trustee William C. Temple had the solution: he would arrange for Rube Waddell to come to Winter Park in January and play for Rollins to overpower the Stetson batters. Temple owned a professional football team as well as the Alleghenies baseball team, now known as the Pittsburgh Pirates, and he was familiar with Waddell. The only problem was the Rollins catcher, who couldn't handle Waddell's powerful fastball. The pitcher insisted he needed a Major League catcher, and Schreck was brought to the campus. That pleased Waddell, not only because he would have his regular catcher but also because he would have his regular drinking buddy.

They each signed up for at least one college course to make them legitimate students, although Schreck was reported to have attended his classes more

The 1903 Rollins College baseball team photo includes Rube Waddell. Seated second from the left is the future Hall of Famer.

often than his flaky teammate. When Stetson players arrived for the game in 1903, they took one look at Waddell in his Rollins uniform, recognized him and caught the next train back to DeLand to avoid embarrassment. The Rollins baseball team won ten of thirteen games that year and considered itself the intercollegiate champion of Florida.

Later that spring, the two pros left Rollins to join their Athletics teammates at spring training in Jacksonville, where Waddell's eccentric behavior continued. He would disappear for days at a time only to be found wrestling an alligator or leading a parade through downtown Jacksonville. He got married to the second of his four wives after knowing her for three days and was arrested on bigamy charges—he had neglected to divorce his first wife. During a game in July, he was suspended by the league for entering the stands to beat up a spectator, and on August 25, his manager suspended him for the rest of the season because he was scheduled to pitch and didn't show up.

A CAREER ON THE SLIDE

With the summer ending early, Waddell went on tour with a theatrical troupe in the melodrama *The Stain of Guilt* and garnered critical acclaim not for his acting but for his ability to toss a villain across the stage. He was eventually fired over money, and his luggage was dumped in an alley.

Waddell led the A's to the 1905 World Series but was unable to pitch because he injured his shoulder near the end of the season in a fight with a teammate. His inability to play fueled rumors that he was paid to miss the series. He was defended by Mack, but his career began to nosedive, and he was traded to the St. Louis Browns.

By this time, Waddell's drinking was out of control, and he passed out on the pitcher's mound during a game in 1909. He was released by St. Louis in 1910. After a brief stint in Newark, he moved to a minor-league team in Minneapolis, living with the team's manager on a farm in Kentucky along the Mississippi River. When a winter flood threatened the town in 1912, Waddell's heroic impulses led him to stand in the icy water up to his armpits for thirteen hours, stacking sandbags. He came down with pneumonia, which led to tuberculosis, and although he pitched for two more seasons, his health continued to deteriorate.

Waddell entered a sanitarium in San Antonio at the end of 1913. He died at age thirty-seven on April Fool's Day in 1914. When Schreck heard about his friend's death, he reportedly said, "The Rube is gone. I am all in. I might as well join him." He died a few months later on July 9, 1914.

Both men were part of a colorful chapter in the history of sports at Rollins College, but they were never recognized as college players who made it to the Majors. Perhaps they should be listed as Major League players who made it to college.

This article first appeared in the February 2010 issue of Winter Park Magazine. *The team photo appears courtesy of the Department of College Archives and Special Collections, Olin Library, Rollins College, Winter Park, Florida.*

Chapter 12

ROLLINS ALUMNUS MAJORED IN ADVENTURE

Author's Life Was the Stuff That Inspires Novels

An hour to the northeast on Interstate 4 lies what is promoted as the World's Most Famous Beach, a broad stretch of oceanside sand at Daytona Beach. So Winter Park's Most Famous Beach also must be a place to swim and sun, right? Not even close. Winter Park's beach was Rex Beach, a Rollins College alumnus and, for most of his life, a prolific and well-known author.

Rex Ellingwood Beach was born September 1, 1877, in Atwood, Michigan, the third son of fruit farmer Henry Walter Beach and his wife, former schoolteacher Eva Eunice Canfield. Henry was a robust, barrel-chested man who delivered Rex with his own hands and possessed almost legendary strength. It's said that he once lifted a grain-filled wagon pulled by four horses to save young Rex, who had fallen under one of its wheels.

In his autobiography, *Personal Exposures*, Rex recalled that his parents were criticized for wanting to educate their boys and send them to college, which was threatening to "the very cornerstone of the local farm-relief program." Henry and Eva had traveled from New York to the Missouri River in a covered wagon in search of a better life and wound up in Michigan. Rural families were large, and boys were especially valued as a built-in labor force to work the farms. Eva, however, envisioned a different future for her sons. She wrote poetry and was well educated for a woman. She was ambitious, not for herself but for her sons, and encouraged their intellectual development. The harsh winters eventually took their toll on Henry. One frigid night, after spending eighteen hours delivering a ton of baled hay, he clawed the ice out of his beard and declared that he had had enough of "Michigan and all points north," his son later wrote. "A man was an idiot to live where his whiskers froze, and once spring arrived he would eat his felt boots, if necessary, but never again would he wear them." It didn't matter to him where they went, and he suggested Eva grab a map of the United States, "stick a pin in that part of it which hung down lowest" and that is where they would be by next fall. Eva "studied the map and liked the color of Florida," and they began to plan the trip.

A TASTE OF ADVENTURE

Several other families wanted to go with them, with one man offering the use of his fishing vessel for their journey. They remodeled the small boat to accommodate eighteen adults and three children, and the travelers began their arduous 103-day voyage through Lake Michigan to the Chicago River, and then down the Illinois and Michigan Canal to the Illinois River and finally to the Mississippi River and the Gulf of Mexico. To a wide-eyed seven-year-old, the trip was amazing, and Rex got his first taste of adventure. Even a fall into the murky Chicago River couldn't dampen his spirits.

As they approached the coast of Florida, many of the adults began shedding layers of clothing in anticipation of a tropical paradise—only to arrive in Tampa in the middle of the worst freeze in forty years. Someone commented that perhaps they should go back to Michigan to thaw out, but the Beach family stayed and began their life in Florida in a drafty tent. They soon moved into a three-room, poorly ventilated house that they shared "with a nocturnal horde of cockroaches, some of which were too large to enter without knocking," before moving into a small cottage, Rex wrote. Henry farmed the Florida soil, and the family worked hard with no luxuries. They ate only what they could not sell and had to be very industrious, which caused some resentment in Rex. "Of all the virtues, industry was the most revolting and frugality ran second." Rex "yearned to be a spendthrift" and especially loathed economizing where food was concerned, claiming he was away at boarding school when he first tasted "the flavor of a banana that had not turned black in the face."

A MOVE TO WINTER PARK

Rex hoped to attend the University of Michigan as his brothers had, but instead he began prep school at Rollins College in 1891 when he was fourteen "for the same reason I ate bananas—it was cheap and I was told it would give me all I needed." Rex became an extremely active student, drawn to both science and literature, and was very involved with the student newspaper, the *Sandspur*. An all-around athlete, Rex was the captain of the Rollins baseball team, a member of the track and field squad and president of the school's tennis club. He served as director of the Athletic Association—and then secretary and treasurer—while still a student.

The busy athlete also was involved in campus academic activities. Rex was a member and later the treasurer of one of the school's literary societies, the Demosthenic Society, and was its president in 1894. At the commencement exercises that year, Rex presented the valedictory address and remained at Rollins until 1896, but he did not finish his degree. In his final months at the school, the *Sandspur* published two of his short stories.

It did not matter that Rex Beach was younger than his college-level teammates. He was stronger and faster (whether on land or in the water) and excelled at any sport in which he competed.

Rex was sure he would follow his brothers and become a lawyer, join their firm as a partner and "then become a Justice of the Supreme Court and live in Washington. There being nine Justices and only one President it looked like a cinch. Furthermore I have always wanted to own a black lounging robe," he wrote in his autobiography.

Rex went to Chicago and began to study law, working at his brothers' firm until the summer of 1897, when gold was discovered along Alaska's Klondike River. After reading accounts of buried riches, Rex decided to take a year off from his studies and "scurry up to Alaska and excavate a fortune." He returned to law school in the winter, but his "blood chemistry had changed. It was the salmon in me no doubt; an upstream urge driving me back to the spawning grounds. Anyhow I no longer had the desire to wear a Supreme Court parka."

Career Path Wanders

The experience proved to be the beginning of his literary career. "A real-life melodrama involving ownership of some of the richest mines in the district was being played and as a consequence when the time came to write his first novel, *The Spoilers*, its plot was ready to use. About all I had to do was add a little imagination, flavor with love interest, season to taste and serve."

For several years, Rex searched for gold and tried many different jobs hoping to improve his luck. During those years, "it was fun to experiment with life, trying a little of this with a pinch of that to see how it would taste. Eventually, however, I began to suspect that I lacked not only what it took to be a lawyer but also what is required to make a miner." He had been dividing his time between mining in Alaska and studying law and brick manufacturing in Chicago. He realized that five years had passed, "leaving me an old man of twenty-four."

After Rex returned to Chicago, he briefly considered selling life insurance but wound up working as a salesman for a brick plant. He began to write seriously, and his first story, "The Mule Boy and the Garrulous Mute," was published in *McClure's Magazine* in 1903. *The Spoilers* was published and became a bestseller in 1906, earning him a reputation as the "Victor Hugo of the North."

In 1904, Rex was a member of the Chicago Athletic Club's water polo team that won a silver medal at the Olympic summer games in St. Louis.

That made him the first person from Rollins to win an Olympic medal. In 1907, Rex married Edith Greta Crater, whose sister, Allene Crater, later married Broadway actor Fred Stone.

BACK TO ROLLINS

Rex returned to Rollins in 1927 for the inauguration of President Hamilton Holt and was presented with an honorary doctorate of literature and the bachelor of science that he hadn't previously completed. He served as the president of the Rollins Alumni Association from 1927 until 1940 and then was its honorary president until 1946.

Rex and Edith retired to Sebring, where he became involved in the experimental farming of celery and flower bulbs. He was popular with Hollywood studios: forty-five movies were made of his thirty-seven novels, plays and stories. His writing continued but at a slower pace than in his earlier years. His health began to decline, followed by Edith's death in 1947, from which he never recovered. Rex developed throat cancer that same year, which eventually led to the insertion of a breathing tube in his neck and another in his stomach for nourishment. His vision was beginning to fail.

Two and a half years after Edith's death, Rex died on December 7, 1949, in his Sebring home reportedly from a self-inflicted gunshot wound. In 2005, that home was being remodeled, and a bullet found in the wall was believed to be the one that ended his life.

Rex Beach is forever linked with Rollins College. The mixed ashes of Rex and Edith were interred on the campus in 1951 near a marble marker close to the Alumni House, and his original manuscripts and correspondence are housed at the college. In 1957, a residence hall designed by John T. Watson was built along Holt Avenue just east of the Knowles Memorial Chapel and named in honor of Winter Park's Most Famous Beach.

This article first appeared in the December 2009 issue of Winter Park Magazine. *The photo of Rex Beach appears courtesy of the Department of College Archives and Special Collections, Olin Library, Rollins College, Winter Park, Florida.*

Chapter 13

FRUITFUL HAPPENSTANCE

The Juicy Story of Florida's Sweet Temple Orange

Merriam-Webster's Online Dictionary defines luck as the "force that brings good fortune or adversity; the events or circumstances that operate for or against an individual." Without a little luck and some bad weather, we might not be enjoying the sweet and juicy Temple orange today.

Known by agriculturalists as a tangor, the fruit originated in Jamaica in the late 1890s and is a cross between a tangerine and an orange. After the severe freezes in Florida during 1894 and 1895, a fruit buyer named Boyce, who regularly supplied northern markets with oranges from Oviedo, traveled to Jamaica for his supply in 1896 because Florida's crop was ruined. He found a notable orange during his search and brought budwood (a shoot of a plant used for grafting) back to Central Florida.

A JAMAICAN TRANSPLANT

Oviedo resident Butler Boston, a leader in the black community, grafted it to trees in area groves. Several years later, budwood from one of those groves was grafted to trees in the Winter Park grove belonging to John Wyeth. After his death, his executor sold the property in 1910 to John and Mary Hakes of New York—despite Mary's vehement objections—while they were on a winter vacation in Florida. The grove was primarily orange trees but included tangerines and grapefruit. Mary tried to persuade John to sell the property, but after three seasons of profitable citrus sales, she changed her mind and agreed it should be kept in the family.

Their son, Louis, and his wife, Ethel, managed the property. In an article Ethel wrote for the *Florida Grower* about fifty years later, she explained, "My husband Louis was then employed by a New York real estate firm, and I was teaching in one of that city's public schools. By the process of elimination, we were picked as the ones to go to Florida. Eventually persuaded, we resigned our jobs and moved to Winter Park." They arrived in December 1913.

EXOTIC FIND

Louis and Ethel were inexperienced but fascinated as they inspected the seventeen-acre grove. Louis noticed an unusual single tree along the driveway that "bore fruit distinctly different from the ordinary orange. Its color was deeper, the pulp tenderer, and the flavor exotic," Ethel wrote. He also noticed that the skin peeled easily, almost as easily as that of a tangerine.

While his father had noticed fruit from that tree was different from that of other trees, he hadn't recognized its value. In previous years, John sold his citrus before the Christmas holidays. Unaware that tangors took longer to mature, John was harvesting that fruit at the same time as other fruit and before it was fully ripe. Luckily, Louis waited until later in the season to market all of the fruit, and the tangor was at its peak.

Recognizing his inexperience in the citrus industry, Louis wanted to find out if this orange was truly valuable. He showed it to other growers, who agreed that the unusual fruit might have commercial potential. He then turned to the man considered the top citrus expert in Florida, William Chase Temple, who happened to be his neighbor.

THE RIGHT PLACE AT THE RIGHT TIME

Temple was born in Starke in 1862 and was educated in Delaware, where his family lived before moving to Florida. He began his professional career in Milwaukee before moving to New York and later Pittsburgh to make his fortune in the steel industry. He improved revenues and business practices in several industries, including iron, steel and coal.

In 1898, Temple returned to Florida and bought an estate overlooking Lake Maitland. He named it "Alabama," and the property included a large home and an orange grove. He and wife Carrie lived in the 1878 Victorian-style home located on the present site of the Alabama Condominiums, formerly the Alabama Hotel. Temple was deeply involved in the community and served as the mayor of Winter Park. He was founder and president of the Board of Trade, a predecessor of the chamber of commerce, and a generous donor and trustee of Rollins College.

Temple's organizational abilities were applied to all of his business ventures. He had invested in several orange groves in Florida and found the state's citrus industry in disarray, with individual growers competing with each other. The groves were poorly managed, and fruit often was rushed to market to cash in on higher prices during the early part of the season.

An Exchange of Ideas

That backfired as consumers were disappointed by the poor quality of the fruit, and profits declined. Temple believed that a cooperative approach could benefit all the growers by implementing better growing practices and standards of quality. A contingent of Florida citrus growers spearheaded by Temple traveled west to study the California Citrus Exchange. They swapped ideas and came back to form the Florida Citrus Exchange in 1909, with Temple serving as president until 1913.

Louis Hakes was lucky to have a well-known citrus authority living practically next door. After sampling the fruit, Temple told Hakes that he had "a valuable find in this orange" and advised him to send a box to the Buckeye Nurseries of Tampa to "put it in the hands of the best citrus nursery in the state," according to Ethel's article. At the same time, Temple wrote to his friend, Myron Gillett, the nursery's owner, to encourage him to examine the fruit.

Gillett was impressed with the rich color of the skin, the ease with which it peeled and the tender, tasty pulp. He traveled to Winter Park and, in 1916, bought the rights to all the budwood produced by the original tree. In exchange, the Hakes family was to receive a royalty of two dollars for each tree sold for the first three years after they were placed on the market.

At first they were told they would have to wait for three years to determine whether budwood from the original tree would produce the desired fruit to receive any payments. The Hakes were thrilled to find that they would not have to wait after all—luckily, another local grower whose trees had been budded from the same tree several years earlier already was producing the new fruit.

Gillett's son and business partner, D. Collins Gillett, wanted to protect Buckeye's exclusivity in marketing the new fruit, which required a government patent. That required a name for the variety. The Gilletts asked if they should use "Hakes," but because the name "was neither euphonious nor of any significance to citrus men," Louis declined, according to Ethel. Temple proposed the "Winter Park Hybrid," but that also was rejected.

IT'S ALL IN THE NAME

Edgar Wright, editor of the popular agricultural magazine the *Florida Grower*, suggested the new orange be named after William Temple because of his reputation in the citrus industry and because he had played a major role in getting the hybrid from the small Winter Park grove to a major nursery where it could be marketed. The name was immediately and enthusiastically accepted, and Buckeye Nurseries publicly announced the availability of the Temple orange in May 1919. It was a fitting tribute to the late William Temple, who had died January 9, 1917.

Articles in daily newspapers as well as the *Florida Grower* turned the original Temple tree in the Hakes's grove into an attraction both for those growing oranges and ordinary tourists, making it one of the early tourist attractions in the state. To protect the tree, a ten-foot wire mesh fence was built around it, further fueling visitors' curiosity.

That single tree is estimated to have produced more than seven million descendants. The Temple orange peaked in popularity from the 1940s into the 1970s. Freezes in later years reduced the number of trees, but the fruit remains popular today. With a little more luck, the Temple will be available for future generations.

This article first appeared in the November 2009 issue of Winter Park Magazine.

Chapter 14

PEACEFUL PRESERVE

Busy Town Has an Oasis of Calm in Genius Drive

Early settlers arriving in what would become Winter Park in the 1880s were enchanted by its natural beauty. As the town grew, they preserved as much of the beautiful wilderness as possible by incorporating parks into their plans. Nearly fifty years later, one man envisioned a peaceful refuge not far from the heart of the city—his dream became Genius Drive.

By 1904, Chicago industrialist and philanthropist Charles Hosmer Morse had become Winter Park's largest landowner, buying property for investment as well as for personal use. Upon his retirement in 1915, his winter home in Winter Park became his primary residence. Morse, who wanted the town to retain the charm and grace that had first attracted him, donated land for Central Park and insisted it be used permanently as a public park. He felt the character of the town was much more important than potential profits.

In 1920, Morse bought land along the shores of Lakes Mizell, Berry and Virginia that had been settled by David Mizell in 1858. The settlement, first known as Lake View and renamed Osceola in 1870, was included within the original town limits of Winter Park. Morse kept nearly two hundred acres undeveloped to provide a refuge from the hustle and bustle of the growing city. According to the *Genius Reserve Guide Book*, he "understood the therapeutic value of nature to humans—that it can provide a sanitary experience that will restore and inspire the observer; that it offers a valuable escape from the push of urban existence." A dirt road was built along the

Charles Morse was a promoter of Winter Park's growth, but he knew it was best to set aside an area to preserve its more natural state. He and his family kept the Genius Drive property from becoming just another subdivision, and a portion of it still retains its natural beauty.

southern half of the Lake Mizell shoreline that included intentional twists and turns designed to prolong the experience for visitors.

To add to the ambience, Morse planted citrus groves, azaleas and other flowering trees and ornamental shrubs. When he died the following year in 1921, a friend sent a note to his daughter, Elizabeth, praising her father and stating, "He had a character that will be an inspiration to his children, his grandchildren, and his great-grandchildren for years to come." Thanks to his daughter and his granddaughter, Jeannette, his legacy continued.

Jeannette was born in 1909 in Chicago, the second child of art lovers Elizabeth Morse and Richard Genius, and she grew up in a refined, artistic atmosphere. Elizabeth was an amateur painter and avid art collector, and she had a great influence on her daughter. Jeannette began her education in private schools in Chicago and Massachusetts and then studied art and interior design in New York. She was on her way to becoming a respected artist, and her work was later featured in museums in New York, New Hampshire, Ohio, Switzerland and France.

IN HER FATHER'S FOOTSTEPS

In 1926, Jeannette enrolled in the summer session at Rollins College. She had visited Winter Park as a child and had indelible memories of time spent with her grandfather at Osceola Lodge, the home he had renovated. Jeannette chose to follow in his footsteps, giving back to the community she loved, and she became a member of the Rollins College Board of Trustees in 1936. That same year, her family finished building Wind Song, a Spanish Renaissance–style home designed by James Gamble Rogers II on the shore of Lake Virginia, across from Rollins. The house was on the

Even though the Dinky Line trains stopped running more than four decades ago, a portion of the old railroad bed can still be seen within the Genius Reserve. This portion is just a few feet from the southern shore of Lake Virginia.

winding dirt road that the family had named Genius Drive in honor of Elizabeth, who died in 1928.

The Winter Park Land Company managed the nearly two-mile-long road, and Jeannette became the company's president in 1941. A gardening staff of about a dozen was employed, and the road was open to the public. Visitors who drove along the picturesque dirt road where trees formed a natural canopy had a view of Winter Park that was much the same as that of the first settlers.

The entrance to Genius Drive was easily reached from Osceola Avenue by going south on Henkel Circle—a distance of just a few blocks but a world away from the paved streets of the city with its traffic and rows of homes. Plant enthusiasts went to see the tall grandiflora magnolias, wild lantanas and red and purple bougainvilleas, as well as scarlet hibiscus, red calliandra and a citrus grove. For many years, the area supervisor was Harold A. Ward, who lived on the property with his family in a large wooden home surrounded by orange trees.

THE PEACOCKS ARRIVE

Native plants were emphasized, but the colorful trees and shrubs added by Morse enhanced the beauty of Genius Drive. Native wildlife was abundant and included gopher tortoises, white-tailed deer, foxes, raccoons, river otters, marsh rabbits and alligators. Bird lovers arrived to observe bald eagles, cooters, red-shouldered and red-tailed hawks, ospreys, barred owls and many other winged species. But Genius Drive earned most of its reputation in the latter part of the century for its peacock population, its most famous transplant.

Visitors came from quite a distance to see more than one hundred colorful peacocks that freely wandered the area. The birds were descendants of those brought to Winter Park by Jeannette and her husband, Hugh McKean. Hugh was an artist and an art professor at Rollins, and he married Jeannette on June 28, 1945. The future Rollins president had become interested in the birds while on a trip to Asia and had them imported to Winter Park in 1950. The McKeans planned to have them live in their front yard along Interlachen Avenue but soon realized how noisy peacocks could be. To maintain peace and quiet in the neighborhood, the peacocks were moved to Genius Drive.

Jeannette and Hugh followed the peacocks the following year when they inherited and moved into Wind Song, also known as Villa Genius, where Jeannette continued her efforts to protect her grandfather's vision. She was honored with an award from *Holiday* magazine, which praised her for "protecting the special personality of the town…creating gardens and a wildlife sanctuary…and for resisting commercial encroachment." Jeannette and Hugh paid further tribute to Morse in 1942 when they opened the Morse Gallery of Art, now the Charles Hosmer Morse Museum of American Art.

Beginning in 1981, the McKeans limited access to Genius Drive, allowing the public to visit only on Sundays. Peacocks had been injured, and orange trees had been damaged. Despite rabies warnings, visitors fed animals by hand. Hundreds of cars crowded the road, encouraged by guidebooks that listed it as one of the best places to visit in Winter Park.

Genius Drive was closed to the public in 1987 because of increased concerns over vandalism and liability. The move was intended to be temporary, but Hugh expressed concern at the time that they "would probably need an endless number of guards" for security that would not only be costly, but they would also spoil the appearance of its natural beauty. Genius Drive was permanently closed to the public in the 1990s.

According to Hugh, it was Jeannette's wish to preserve the land her grandfather had set aside. "She feels that if the remaining natural land is broken up, everybody in Winter Park will suffer some," he said. Jeannette died in 1989, and despite her desire to preserve the property, 152 acres were sold a decade later for home sites. What remains undeveloped is roughly one-fourth of the original wilderness owned and cherished by Charles Morse. Hugh died in 1995.

That land is now known as the Genius Reserve and is part of a restoration project by the Department of Environmental Studies of Rollins College; it serves as an outdoor classroom for Rollins students. It includes the largest remaining orange grove within Winter Park's city limits and several structures, including Wind Song.

Walking paths include a portion of the Dinky Line rail bed, near the south shore of Lake Mizell, and the pignut hickory-lined Jeannette's Walk, near the north shore of Lake Berry where Jeannette often strolled. On a quiet day, the calls of peacocks can still be heard through the locked gates at the ends of the reserve or along the lakes that attracted the first settlers to Winter Park more than 150 years ago.

This article first appeared in the January 2010 issue of Winter Park Magazine. *The photo of Charles Morse appears courtesy of the First Congregational Church of Winter Park. The other photo was taken by the authors.*

Chapter 15

Winter Park's "Delightful Resort"

A Lodging with Class and Privacy

W hen drivers enter Winter Park, they are met by signs that say "Please drive with extraordinary care." The intention may be to protect the residents who live along narrow tree-lined streets, but it also gives visitors an opportunity to view elegant buildings and extraordinary neighborhoods. If structures could talk, they would give an account of Winter Park's past, but none would have more to say than the Alabama Hotel. Its storied history is as rich and varied as the clientele it originally served.

The property was first owned by an early Winter Park settler, Thomas J. Mathers, who in 1876 bought 154 acres on the south side of Lake Maitland from the U.S. government for the lofty price of $1.25 per acre. In 1898, William C. Temple bought the lakefront property, which included an estate and a large orange grove. He named it Alabama, an Indian word meaning "clearing for encampment" or "place of rest."

He and his wife, Carrie, sold the land in 1915 to Herbert Halverstadt of Pennsylvania, who sold it to Helen E. Sherman of Maine in 1917. She then sold it in 1920 to Joseph and Anna Kronenberger of Ohio, who formed the Alabama Hotel Co. with plans to build a resort attracting northern visitors to the area, much as the Seminole Hotel had until it burned nearly two decades earlier. The Kronenbergers were looking for more than just guests to fill their hotel, however. Their goal was to sell them home sites in their planned Kronenberger Subdivision.

The large Temple house was moved northeastward from its original location to make room for the hotel and is today part of the stately condominium complex.

ROOMS WITH A VIEW

But they needed a luxury hotel. The Temple family home was moved a little to the northeast in 1921 to provide a large empty lot, and the Kronenbergers began building a four-story, eighty-room structure based on the California Mission architectural style. The thirty-thousand-square-foot hotel essentially was completed in 1922, with amenities that included steam heat and telephones in rooms, a private beach along Lake Maitland and boats for hotel guests. There was a full dining room with a lounge featuring a grand piano.

The hotel lacked only the final coat of stucco, which was never applied by the Kronenbergers. They had leased the hotel to D.L. Rice and F.B. Lynch in 1923, but the Kronenbergers' company declared bankruptcy in May of that year, and the court-appointed trustee, William B. Crawford, was ordered to sell the property. Clifford Folger of Nantucket, Massachusetts, bought the buildings and surrounding land in 1924 for $100,900.

Clifford and his brother, Fred H. Folger, also owned a hotel in Nantucket. They developed financial troubles, and when the stock market crashed in 1929, the brothers decided to keep only one of their properties—the Nantucket hotel.

The Alabama passed into the hands of the bondholders and was neglected for several years, according to a detailed book written by Noella La Chance Schenck, who first saw the hotel in October 1932. She and her husband, Henry Schenck, had driven to Winter Park from Michigan with her father, E.J. La Chance, and her brother, Gene, to see the property after her father was asked if he wanted to run the hotel for the 1933 season.

E.J. and his family had gained experience operating the Grand Hotel in Mackinac Island in Michigan for the summer of 1932. Although he had sold his interest in the resort several years earlier, E.J. was asked to return and run it for the summer. Henry Schenck had lost his position as a teaching assistant while studying for his doctorate degree, so he and Noella joined the family in the successful operation of the resort.

ROAD TRIP

At the end of the season, E.J. received a letter from Alabama Hotel bondholders in Winter Park, which he dismissed as a Florida scam and tossed in the trash. Gene joked that they should consider the offer because of the climate, and Henry retrieved the letter from the wastebasket, believing it to be a good opportunity. After a lengthy discussion, E.J. offered to foot the bill for a quick trip to Florida with his son and son-in-law if they would drive his Studebaker. Noella said "not without me," and they left two days later.

After meeting with bondholders, E.J. and his family understood why no one had been found to run the resort. Bondholders' demands were high: a one-year lease with a lump sum payment in advance. Few people had the resources or the desire to take such a risk in 1933, in addition to having the money required to get the hotel ready to reopen. The family toured the property again and then went back up north, assuring bondholders that they would review the proposal and make a decision quickly.

Relying heavily on Gene's financial expertise, they agreed to lease the hotel for the coming year. Gene remained with his accounting firm in Chicago, and Noella and Henry moved to Winter Park to run the hotel with her father.

FINANCIAL CRISIS AVOIDED

Shortly after they opened, President Roosevelt announced the closing of the banks on March 6, 1933. Hotel guests were nervous and uncertain as to how they would pay their bills, but Henry allowed them to write checks and persuaded a local bank to hold them until the guests' banks reopened. He assured guests that the hotel would continue to provide meals and that they had "a fairly good supply of food in our storerooms and freezers." Noella organized a well-catered party, and their kindness turned out to be an excellent business decision. The hotel didn't lose any money once banks opened a week later.

E.J. and Henry signed a contract to buy the hotel in the spring of 1935, contingent upon the application of the final coat of stucco by the bondholders. After her father's death, Noella inherited his one-half interest, and she and Henry continued to own and operate the hotel until 1960. Noella's influence could be seen throughout the hotel, from the art in the lobby, to the extensive library and to the beautiful flatware, linens and china used every day for meals, including a high tea served weekdays.

A SOUTHERN DELIGHT

Brochures described the Alabama as "one of the most delightful resorts in the South" and promised "a widely diversified social life enlivened by the presence of sportsmen, artists, writers, scholars and statesmen of national and international note." Notable guests included orchestra conductor Leopold Stokowski and authors Thornton Wilder, Harlow Shapley, Sinclair Lewis and Margaret Mitchell. But unlike some resorts where celebrities would go to be seen, the Alabama was a wooded retreat where they could seek peace and quiet.

Mitchell and her husband were visiting their friend Edwin Granberry in Winter Park in 1938. She was easily recognized after *Gone With the Wind* was published, so Granberry took them to the Alabama, and the Schencks registered them under another name to ensure their privacy.

The Schencks sold the hotel in 1960 to a group of five Winter Park men led by Paul E. Sharts. They abandoned their plans for redeveloping the property and continued to operate the hotel until 1979, when it was sold to Sam Azarian of Wisconsin.

Azarian sold it in January of the following year to Alabama Development Inc., led by Charles M. Simmerson and Charles Booth. They renovated the eighty-unit hotel on Alabama Drive into a twenty-unit luxury condominium, leaving the original barn and garage intact. They also kept the Temple Refectory built by William C. Temple in 1904.

Even with all the changes made to the hotel over the years, the outside looks today very much as it did in old photos and postcards. The columns and the front walls of the building are covered with thick vines reminiscent of olden days.

This article first appeared in the August 2009 issue of Winter Park Magazine. *The photo was taken by the authors.*

Chapter 16

A Different Breed
of College President

Nonconformist Beliefs Set Rollins on Path of Excellence

Many college presidents have extensive backgrounds in education and are selected based on academic credentials. Not so in the case of Hamilton Holt, the unlikely eighth president of Rollins College, who once said, "No person or institution can educate anybody. All true education is self-education."

Holt was born in Brooklyn in 1872. His father, a distinguished Yale graduate and the valedictorian of his Columbia College Law School class, was a liberal independent thinker with high integrity who greatly influenced his son. His mother, a gifted musician with a passion for reading, encouraged her son's development. Holt pursued many interests, including music and baseball. He was never quite the star student, but he studied diligently and maintained relatively good grades. Expecting to follow in his father's footsteps, Holt began his college career at Yale in 1890. Unfortunately, he found himself in the bottom third of his class, and "Old Grouch," as his friends and classmates nicknamed him, became withdrawn. He was mostly unsuccessful in extracurricular activities, and none of his writing was published in the student magazine his father had edited.

According to a biography written by Rollins graduate Warren F. Kuehl, Holt later said that his college years "had neither educated nor developed him." His education really began in 1894 with a part-time job at his grandfather's magazine, the *Independent*, during graduate school at Columbia College. Holt knew nothing of the publishing business when he began work,

Hamilton Holt stood out from the crowd when it came to his words and his actions. As a result, Rollins College was transformed into something different from a typical liberal arts college, providing a unique educational opportunity.

but he was surrounded by intelligent and savvy businessmen, and he soon developed into a fine editor. A year after the death of his grandfather in 1896, Holt became a full-time journalist and quit graduate school, lacking only his dissertation. Holt became the magazine's managing editor and blossomed into a self-confident, dynamic young man.

HIGH IDEALS

Under Holt's guidance, many changes were instituted, and the *Independent* expanded from a religious journal into a publication of general interest that featured articles from some of the nation's best minds. By 1912, the

Independent was regarded as one of the best weekly publications in the country, and Holt bought it from his uncle and spent most of the next decade at its helm. During those years, Holt was not afraid to use the *Independent* as a platform for his high ideals. For more than two decades, he pursued the development of an international organization to promote world peace. He was instrumental in securing a $10 million donation from Andrew Carnegie to establish the Carnegie Endowment for International Peace in 1910. That same year, Holt delivered an address, titled "The Federation of the World," at Rollins College; he was invited by Rollins president William F. Blackman to join the board of trustees in 1914 and served for two years.

Facing declining revenues from the 1920 recession, the magazine folded in 1921 and Holt retired as editor. President Warren G. Harding's refusal to support Holt's impassioned campaign to allow the United States to join the League of Nations (a predecessor to the United Nations) led to Holt's decision to switch political parties. A special election was held in 1924 when a Republican senator in Connecticut committed suicide, and Holt ran as a Democrat, hoping to establish a wider base of support for the league. The traditionally Republican state was dominated by a ruthless party machine, and Holt lost the election.

By 1925, he had begun to tire of his campaign for the League of Nations. Long lecture tours and a stressful political campaign had taken their toll on his health, and he began to look for other ways to make a living. He wrote to friends in Florida for advice. One of those friends was novelist Irving Bacheller, a Winter Park resident and trustee of Rollins College who extended an interesting offer: the presidency of the college with an annual salary of $5,000, plus a home. It was tempting, especially considering Holt's health, and his wife urged him to accept. But he wasn't sure his background had prepared him for an academic setting. Holt replied with his own proposal: he would take the job on a trial basis starting in December at the $5,000 salary, which would give him time to honor other commitments and to develop a plan for the college. If the board wanted him to continue after the first of May, he would require a salary of no less than $10,000 a year and a home. The trustees met during the summer and accepted his proposal that September.

SEARCHING FOR A BETTER WAY

Holt set himself a lofty goal: to transform Rollins into "an ideal small college." As an editor, he had visited more than three hundred colleges and universities and had determined that teaching methods needed to be revitalized, believing there was a "lack of human contact between teacher and student." Holt no doubt reflected on his own college experience when he concluded that the lecture system was "probably the worst scheme ever devised for imparting knowledge." He realized "that my colleagues in the editorial room, who never thought of teaching me anything, taught me everything, while my professors at Yale and Columbia, who were paid to teach me, taught me virtually nothing."

   Holt sought to re-create the intimate atmosphere he had experienced with his magazine job, and in June 1926, after consulting with individual professors, he proposed a Two-Hour Conference Plan as an experiment to replace the lecture system. The plan allowed small groups of students to meet several times a week and interact with professors in a casual classroom setting instead of a formal lecture hall. The faculty voted unanimously to implement the plan in the fall of 1926. Despite some glitches, the plan was enormously popular with professors and students and helped increase enrollment.

AN INNOVATIVE EDUCATOR

Holt formed a faculty committee to ensure his teaching methods were meeting the needs of individual students. He subsequently invited a group of distinguished educators to attend a curriculum conference in January 1931, hosted by noted professor John Dewey. The recommendations from the conference were implemented that fall, further confirming the status of Rollins College as an innovative institution. Holt utilized his contacts and his publishing experience to promote his teaching methods, and Sinclair Lewis acknowledged the college as the most encouraging campus in the country for contemporary authors in an acceptance speech for the 1930 Nobel Prize in literature. As a result, Holt was able to attract many prominent figures to the campus and was adamant about exposing the student population to "great men who have achieved supremacy in any legitimate line." He introduced the Animated Magazine, an annual series of five-minute minilectures

On display in the Mills Memorial Building is this bronze bust of Hamilton Holt. It was sculpted by Marjorie Daingerfield Holmes, who from 1935 until 1937 was a Rollins College sculpture instructor.

from prominent men and women that attracted thousands of attendees. Holt created the "Walk of Fame," a collection of steppingstones on the campus, representing great men and women of international prominence who had made contributions to mankind. Another of Holt's contributions to the campus was the selection of the Spanish Mediterranean style of architecture. He believed an attractive environment played an essential role in an educational institution's success, and twenty-three new buildings were added during Holt's administration.

In spite of various controversies, Holt's presidency was considered successful. He was beloved by faculty and students and inspired great loyalty. He was affectionately referred to as "Prexy" by his admirers. He retired in 1949 after serving as president for twenty-four years. He died in the family home in Woodstock, Connecticut, in 1951.

Hamilton Holt was a complex man who experienced many failures in a lifetime of successes. His legacy at Rollins can still be seen in its beautiful architecture on the campus, and it is still felt in the teaching methods he encouraged. He was a practical idealist who set often-unattainable goals for himself—but in striving to achieve them, he accomplished much.

This article first appeared in the June 2009 issue of Winter Park Magazine. *The photo of Hamilton Holt appears courtesy of the Department of College Archives and Special Collections, Olin Library, Rollins College, Winter Park, Florida. The photo of the bust of Hamilton Holt was taken by the authors.*

Chapter 17

ROLLINS'S ANIMATED MAGAZINE

Program Brought Culture, News to Life

Hamilton Holt, one of the most beloved presidents in the history of Rollins College, also was one of the most innovative during his twenty-four-year tenure. He established many programs that lasted for decades, including one that began as a marketing tool. A discussion with a new member of his staff led to the development of the Animated Magazine, an annual event that attracted thousands to the campus.

In 1926, Holt and Edwin Grover, a former publisher with thirty years' experience who had been given the title of professor of books at Rollins, were talking about ways to publicize the college. Holt suggested creating a magazine; Grover suggested an "animated" magazine, with contributors presenting their ideas to a live audience.

Grover's idea appealed to Holt, and he and Grover held the first Animated Magazine in February 1927 during Founders' Week. Rollins students, faculty and staff were joined by local residents and prominent visitors to experience a variety of celebrities performing portions of their works or presenting their opinions on the day's important issues. Often, one or more contributors would be presented with an honorary degree or other award as part of the celebration.

The two men walking down the aisle through the throng of spectators at the 1941 Animated Magazine are Hamilton Holt (in the white suit) and Edwin Osgood Grover. They created the annual event, which was enjoyed by the entire community.

CULTURAL GLITTERATI

The first year's contributors included author and Rollins alumnus Rex Beach, novelists Irving Bacheller and Corra Harris, humorist Opie Read, editors Ed W. Howe and Albert Shaw and poets Cale Young Rice, Jessie Rittenhouse and Clinton Scollard. Held on the shore of Lake Virginia in the open-air Recreation Hall, about six hundred subscribers (audience members) attended and shivered through the program of impressive presenters. Stoves were added the following year, but they did little to provide comfort from a cold rain. Despite the weather, the crowd was too big for the Recreation Hall, and the program was repeated twice more during the day in the Old Chapel and the Congregational church to handle the overflow. For the 1929 edition, the Animated Magazine was turned into a true outdoor event on the campus lawn, and Hamilton Holt promised "hot February sun" for each year's presentation.

For the first three decades, the college printed programs that resembled a four-page magazine. The program included a foreword, an introduction by the president as editor; editorial, a presentation by a contributor; articles, presentations by the rest of the contributors; and an advertisement, usually an invitation to contribute to a worthy campus cause such as the library or a scholarship program. The names of the speakers were arranged like a table of contents, and the masthead initially listed Hamilton Holt as editor and Edwin O. Grover as publisher.

Imitating a printed magazine, it included the following:

Entered at the Rollins College Campus as
"first class matter"

All Rights—but no wrongs—Reserved

Subscription Price—Whatever you ought
to give. All the proceeds of this Animated
Magazine will be devoted to the purchase of
books which are greatly needed for the Rollins
College Library.

Later, the earmarking of the funds for the library was changed to "Student Aid."

CONTRIBUTORS FROM ALL WALKS OF LIFE

Holt and Grover tried to invite a variety of contributors each year. For example, the 1929 presentation included three editors, five poets, four authors of prose, an army general and a New York City church rector. The following year, Dan Beard, one of the founders of the Boy Scouts, made an appearance and returned for another in 1933. Presidents and professors from Mount Holyoke College, the University of Florida and Columbia University were featured.

Government leaders began appearing in 1934, when Florida governor Dave Sholtz delivered the welcome address after Holt's traditional foreword. That same year, the program included the U.S. attorney general and secretary of commerce. In 1941, Governor Spessard Holland was a contributor and a recipient of an honorary degree. Senator Claude Pepper was a speaker at the 1943, 1945 and 1948 Animated Magazines.

Subscribers were treated to excerpts from new or unpublished works read by their authors, often well before they would become famous. One such work was *The Yearling* by Marjorie Kinnan Rawlings (1938).

ACKNOWLEDGING WARTIME

During World War II, Holt was moved to second billing in the Table of Contents. He was preceded by the posting of flags and the singing of the "Star-Spangled Banner" by all in attendance. The war years also introduced another page to the written program; a list of Rollins alumni who were killed in the war was included, and in 1944, the Gold Star Memorial Scholarships, one in memory for each of the twelve men who to that point had died while serving, were added. That number increased to twenty-three and then twenty-six in the next two years.

Invitees continued to include presenters of national prominence. They included J. Edgar Hoover, Bob Feller, Joe Tinker, Leo Durocher, Fred Stone (an actor who had a relationship with Rollins and has a small theater named for him on the campus), Greer Garson, Leo G. Carroll, Edward R. Murrow, Ogden Nash, Edward Everett Horton, Basil Rathbone, Mary Pickford, Lillian Gish, James Cagney, Muhammad Ali, Walter Cronkite, Arnold Palmer, Wernher von Braun and Al Capp. Local personalities included Martin Andersen, publisher of the *Orlando Sentinel*, and Orlando mayor Carl Langford.

The popularity of the Animated Magazine drew tremendous crowds to the outdoor presentation. The number of "subscribers" at the 1949 event was estimated at 8,000, filling the intramural field with chairs as others stood or sat on the grass nearby. Holt and Grover figured that to that point, more than 100,000 subscribers had attended the twenty-two magazines they had produced.

NEW PRESIDENT BRINGS CHANGES

In 1952, new Rollins president Hugh McKean took over as the editor of the Animated Magazine. The format of the printed program was changed for the first time, making it look less like the cover and pages of an issue of

National Geographic and more like a program for a play. For the first time, a photograph appeared—one of Hamilton Holt, to whom the magazine was dedicated. During that decade, Edwin Granberry replaced Edwin Grover as the publisher.

During the 1960s, the list of contributors was shortened, sometimes to as few as four. Less attention was paid to authors, poets, entertainers and athletes, with the emphasis instead on scientists, educators and government officials. What was once a collection of a variety of subjects was turning into a symposium on a specific, serious topic. Attendance waned, and the annual event evolved from a sprawling audience of thousands to one that could fit inside the Knowles Memorial Chapel. Performances by the Men's Choir, Chapel Choir, Rollins Singers and Rollins Chorale were featured in a few of the years.

The 1969 Animated Magazine had a very different format than that which Holt and Grover had established. Instead of a single venue where a large crowd would experience the entire magazine contents from the foreword to the final page, the speakers were scheduled at different hours in various locations, competing with open houses, organ performances and tours throughout the campus.

That year was also the last year of the annual Animated Magazine. The following year, there was none under new president Jack Critchfield. A one-time revival of the event was staged in 1985 during the administration of Thaddeus Seymour for the college's centennial celebration, and another was presented in 2010 for the 125th anniversary of the school's founding, but the "World's Only Magazine That Comes Alive" effectively put out its last issue in 1969.

This article first appeared in the July 2010 issue of Winter Park Magazine. *The photo appears courtesy of the Department of College Archives and Special Collections, Olin Library, Rollins College, Winter Park, Florida.*

Chapter 18

ROLLINS'S WALK OF FAME KEEPS PACE WITH HISTORY

Stones Honor Those Who Shaped the Human Story

A walk through the campus of Rollins College is a walk through history. Look beyond the beautiful Spanish Mediterranean architecture, and you find the Walk of Fame created by Hamilton Holt, president of the college from 1925 to 1949.

Holt had a summer home, Gauge Hall, in Woodstock, Connecticut, which had served as a tavern during the American Revolution and had been in his family for more than six generations. While Hamilton was on vacation in the early 1920s, his father suggested they drive through Massachusetts and Connecticut and search for their ancestors' homesteads.

ROCKS OF AGES

The younger Holt came up with the idea of collecting stones from each of the homesteads, which led to more trips in search of keepsake stones. In a somewhat crude fashion, Hamilton and his sons chiseled into the stones the names of the ancestors and their hometowns and the dates when they lived there. They added them to a walk of steppingstones already in place, forming an interesting "ancestral walk" on the grounds of their Woodstock home.

That walkway was known mainly to Hamilton Holt's close friends and relatives, but he decided to expand the project to include a second walkway with stones dedicated to more widely recognized individuals. When that part of the collection reached about twenty stones, Holt and his wife agreed to donate them to Rollins, and they were shipped from Connecticut to Winter Park.

The Memorial Path of Fame—as it was originally called—was dedicated on October 18, 1929, and the collection of engraved stones was placed in a prominent location along the "Horseshoe," the central part of the original Rollins campus that earned its nickname because of its shape. The twenty-two stones represented individuals who had achieved prominence nationally or internationally. The stones came from their birthplaces, former homes, grave sites or sites associated with them. Original honorees included George Washington, Henry Wadsworth Longfellow, Calvin Coolidge and Ralph Waldo Emerson. Soon afterward, the name was changed to the Walk of Fame, and in less than three months, the collection grew to more than fifty, including stones for Presidents Lincoln, Wilson, Hoover, Jefferson, McKinley, Johnson and Pierce.

ROCK STARS

On trips to New England to raise money for the college, Holt and Vice-President A.J. Hanna visited historic sites to collect stones representing previous residents, such as Daniel Webster. When Holt traveled to Europe, his return luggage was heavy with stones from sites associated with famous figures such as Christopher Columbus, Cervantes, Percy Bysshe Shelley and Benjamin Disraeli.

During the 1930s, the Walk of Fame attracted the interest not only of faculty and students but also of residents of Winter Park. They made it their goal to collect stones whenever they traveled, and they added to the collection notable names such as Buffalo Bill, Washington Irving, Edgar Allan Poe and Horace Mann. By 1931, there were more than two hundred stones laid to the west of Carnegie Hall, with many more yet to be added.

With so many stones being collected, Holt developed guidelines for what could be included. It was his plan to include a monument to "every man or woman, living or dead, whose services deserve the eternal remembrances of mankind." He rejected those whose reputations were unknown outside of a single state, preferring to honor those who were widely known, such as Confucius and William Shakespeare.

Holt solicited stones from around the world. While his requests mostly were granted, on at least two occasions, he was rejected. He asked for a stone to represent Joseph H. Choate, the head of the American Bar Association who had served as an ambassador to Great Britain. His daughter declined to provide a stone from his birthplace in Salem, Massachusetts.

His initial request for a stone to represent the Dionne quintuplets also was turned down. Stones from the grounds of the Ontario hospital where they were born in 1934 had a reputation of enhancing fertility, and there was a flood of requests. That, however, resulted in the hospital deciding not to part with any of the stones. When Holt tried again, he convinced the hospital that Rollins College was interested in the stones for strictly historical matters and not superstition.

Sermons in Stones

The most prominent marker is an upright millstone at the start of the Walk of Fame. Holt found the millstone beside an unused milldam in East Woodstock, Connecticut. The stone had been moved to the side of a road owned by Marcus Morse, the cousin of two Rollins students. Holt bought it and another millstone for a few dollars and hauled them back to his summer home, where they remained for several years. When he decided to present one to the college in 1933, the 3,300-pound stone was trucked to Winter Park by two Rollins students who were paid forty dollars for the 1,200-mile trip. The inscription on the millstone reads: "Sermons in stones and good in everything," a quote from Shakespeare's *As You Like It*.

An important feature of the Walk of Fame collection is the connection each stone has with its human honoree. Each bit of granite or other material must come from a site closely associated with the person, such as the piece of a schoolhouse in which Confucius once taught or the fragment of a crypt in which Columbus was buried for a time in Cuba. Admiral Richard Byrd brought back the stone that represents him on a dogsled from a mountain near the South Pole. The Charles Dickens stone is a piece of flint that had been near a wooden cross he erected to mark the grave of his pet canary.

In 1945, a stone from the bunker fireplace of Adolf Hitler was donated and was accepted by Holt, causing much controversy. Holt stated he "always wanted a Walk of Ill Fame in which to put Benedict Arnold, Madame de

Pompadour, Hitler, Mussolini, and President Harding." He never got the chance to carry out this plan, as the Hitler stone quickly disappeared and was never seen again.

By the early 1950s, the Walk of Fame included more than 800 stones from around the world. When Holt retired in 1949, the project lost its strongest advocate. Not only was there no longer a push to collect more stones, the ones that were there started to vanish. Some were tossed into Lake Virginia as graduation pranks, and others likely became souvenirs of the college campus. Other stones suffered damage from foot traffic and weather, making it difficult to read the person's name in the inscription. One count showed that 179 stones had been taken from the walk, and 33 others had been removed because of damage.

When Thaddeus Seymour became the Rollins president in 1978, one of his goals was to return the dilapidated Walk of Fame to its former prominence. Hamilton Holt himself was formally honored with the dedication of a stone on May 27, 1979. The college designated an official lapidarian to maintain records of the stones, and a firm of landscape architects was hired to preserve the remaining stones.

ROCK ON

Today, there are more than five hundred stones placed in a dozen beds along the Horseshoe bordering the lawn of the Mills Memorial Center. There are stones memorializing twenty-one U.S. presidents, recipients of fourteen Nobel Prizes and individuals from more than thirty-five countries. In addition, there are pieces of historic buildings, the Berlin Wall, the Great Wall of China and the destroyed World Trade Center towers.

Earlier this year, a stone was added honoring Annie Russell, an actress of international fame whose involvement with Rollins College was instrumental in the development of the theater department and the hall that bears her name.

The tradition continues.

This article first appeared in the March 2009 issue of Winter Park Magazine.

Chapter 19

KRAFT AZALEA GARDEN: WHERE NATURE STARS

Park Ranks Among City's Most Beloved Sites

Kraft Azalea Garden on Lake Maitland is one of Winter Park's most beautifully landscaped parks. With eleven acres of tropical plants, majestic trees and thousands of azaleas that blaze with color from January through March, this lovely park on Alabama Avenue attracts residents and visitors looking for a quiet place to relax, as well as those seeking a picturesque venue for an intimate outdoor wedding. The park bears monuments to two men—Leonard J. Hackney and George Kraft—and their contributions to Winter Park and the park.

HACKNEY'S LEGAL LEGACY

Born in Edinburgh, Indiana, Leonard J. Hackney attended neither college nor law school but became a judge in 1888 at age thirty-three in a campaign marred by accusations of fraud and corruption, according to an article by Indiana court historian Judge Margaret Robb. Just four years later, in spite of continued allegations by Republicans of wrongdoing, Democrat Hackney was elevated to the state Supreme Court. He was on that bench for only seven years, but he left a lasting civil rights legacy.

Four months after becoming a justice on the state Supreme Court, he wrote the majority opinion in the case of Antoinette Dakin Leach, reversing the trial court's decision to bar her from becoming a lawyer because, as a woman, she did not have the right to vote. The opinion was celebrated as a victory for women's rights, both in Indiana and throughout the country. It also elevated Hackney's reputation. After leaving the Supreme Court, he became an attorney for the Cleveland, Cincinnati, Chicago & St. Louis Railway Co.

A WINTER PARK TRANSPLANT

In 1925, Hackney moved to Winter Park with his wife of forty-five years, Ida. They lived in Sandscove, a large home at 1461 Via Tuscany, and also had a home built at 1420 Via Tuscany, which they sold in 1929 to actress Annie Russell. Sandscove had a view of an overgrown, unnamed park across Lake Maitland that had been established by 1910 and was listed on a recorded plat simply as a "park." It later was called Alabama Park because William C. Temple's estate across the street was known as Alabama.

Hackney represented the railroad until 1928 when he became a director of the Union State Bank in Winter Park. After the 1929 stock market crash, the state ordered it and other local banks to close to preserve depositors' assets. Hackney was still on the board when George Kraft and Irving Bacheller used their own assets to shore up the bank, allowing it to remain in business under a new name, the Florida Bank at Winter Park. Hackney continued to serve on the board and joined a campaign to improve the park on Alabama Avenue.

KRAFT-ING A GARDEN

George Kraft was a merchant in the Midwest. His Kraft Clothing Co., later known as the Kraft, Odell Clothing Co., had branch stores in several small but prosperous towns, including Fort Madison, Iowa. In 1886, he married Agnes Maud Houston. His Chicago firm, known as the George Kraft Co., in the 1920s owned and operated a chain of five-and-dime stores, which he later sold to the F.W. Woolworth Co. when he was sixty-three. Upon retirement, he and Maud moved to Winter Park in 1927.

When the Krafts arrived in Winter Park, the park along Lake Maitland's south shore had been cleared but not developed. Kraft and a landscape gardener began transplanting azaleas from the Kraft home, which was at the northeast corner of Georgia and Webster Avenues. They cultivated cuttings, and as the shrubs matured, they planted them in the park. Soon after, Alabama Park became known as Azalea Garden and Honor Azalea Garden. Maud served as the chairwoman of the North End Circle of the Winter Park Garden Club, which took an active role in maintaining the park.

PARK TAKES SHAPE

By 1931, the garden was sponsored by the Commercial Club. It hired Orlando nursery owner Martin J. Daetwyler to develop plans for the park's layout, which included walking trails bordered by azaleas and other plants. The park was to be surrounded by a flint rock curb, with decorative rocks every three to four feet. The Azalea Garden Committee, chaired by Leonard Hackney, supervised the transformation of the park into a showplace. Also on the committee were Mrs. H.M. Sinclair, the Garden Club president; Mrs. C.F. Ward, the Woman's Club president; Forney W. Shepherd, a member of the Commercial Club; H.W. Caldwell; and Mayor Frederick W. Cady.

Daetwyler took over much of the planting of the park, and in 1934, the city became responsible for its maintenance. It was renamed Kraft Azalea Garden in 1937 after Kraft died, and the Kraft family promised to pay for the park's care. Maud and her son did just that, allowing it to continue to provide joy to those who came to experience its beauty.

Hackney died October 9, 1938, and the following year, a plaque was attached to a column at the entrance to the gardens, honoring Hackney as the "Creator of the Gardens." The Winter Park City Commission decided that it would be the last such plaque placed in the park, other than trail markers. They did not want the park to be a collection of memorials for prominent Winter Park residents.

ADDING FUNCTION, BEAUTY

In 1946, the Winter Park Garden Club installed a drinking fountain to commemorate an award presented to the club by *Horticulture* magazine. It still functions today.

Steve Prince and Linda Betsinger pause in front of the exedra just after their wedding ceremony. Many couples choose the site along the Lake Maitland shoreline to provide a lovely setting for their special day.

The most striking feature in the park, other than the countless azaleas, is a structure that resembles a portion of an ancient Greek temple. Located near the water, it was erected in 1969–1970 at a cost of $35,000 and was donated by Kenneth H. and Elizabeth P. Kraft to honor George and Maud. They called it an "exedra," a word coined from the Greek "ex" (out) and "hedra" (seat). At eighteen feet wide and fourteen feet tall, it provides a beautiful backdrop for photos. Its inscription reads: "Pause friend let beauty refresh the spirit."

Kraft Azalea Garden has never had restrooms, electrical access, pavilions, playgrounds or barbecue grills. What is does have is beauty and tranquility—a wonderful place to leave the hustle and bustle behind.

This article first appeared in the September 2010 issue of Winter Park Magazine. *The photo of the newlyweds appears courtesy of Steve and Linda Prince.*

Chapter 20

Winter Park's Wonderful Waterways

Lakes, Canals Attract Visitors to City

Apopular attraction in Winter Park is a boat tour through the canals and chain of lakes just east of downtown and Rollins College. During the guided tour, the history of the parks and buildings along the shore is recounted. The beautiful waters became a route for tours beginning in 1938, but the history of the canals and lakes goes back much further.

LAKEFRONT PROPERTY

The earliest settlers in Winter Park were attracted to the cluster of lakes that included Mizell, Osceola and Virginia. David W. Mizell brought his family to the area in 1858 where they established a settlement along the eastern shore of Lake Osceola and appropriately called it Lake View. In 1870, the area was renamed Osceola in honor of a local Seminole Indian chief, and it was later included within the original boundaries of the incorporated town of Winter Park, which was cofounded by Loring A. Chase and Oliver E. Chapman.

When Chase first visited the area in 1881, there was a crude freight platform at the railroad tracks crossing New England Avenue, a convenient loading site for lumber that had been dressed at a sawmill owned by John K. Coiner and located on the north shore of Lake Virginia, which Coiner had named for his home state. As Winter Park developed and the demand for lumber increased, it became more difficult to haul logs longer distances

The Osceola-Maitland Run, turned into a canal connecting Lakes Maitland and Osceola, has been a popular place to paddle and row since the earliest days of Winter Park. Standing all the way to the left is Winter Park founder Loring A. Chase.

on roads, which were little more than dirt paths. The lakes were a natural solution: their proximity to each other made it relatively easy to connect them with canals. Initially, the canals were dug as straight as possible to float logs to be dressed at the mill for construction. By 1881, the Fern Canal connecting Lakes Osceola and Virginia was a regular thoroughfare for timber.

Tourists, especially those staying at the Seminole Hotel, also made use of the lakes during these years. Guests could check out rowboats and explore the area on their own, or they could cruise aboard steam launches, including the *Fanny Knowles*, the *Gussie* and the *May B.* The many lakes and canals made Winter Park a popular tourist attraction.

STABILIZING THE CANALS

The early canals—including the Genius Canal, opened by Coiner in 1875 to connect Lakes Mizell and Virginia—had dirt banks that were susceptible to erosion and limited their usage. That problem led to the installation of

Adjacent to the Rollins College campus is beautiful Lake Virginia, which provides many opportunities for aquatic recreation. Shown here in 1929 is its diving tower, used for competition and fun.

seawalls in the Fern and Venetian Canals. The Venetian connects Lakes Maitland and Osceola. During the 1930s, the Federal Emergency Relief Administration had crews working on several local public projects, including widening and deepening the canals so that larger vessels could safely pass.

The canals have since been allowed to wind a bit through dense foliage, making them more interesting to the eye. There are limits, however, because the canals still need to accommodate water traffic for sightseers, fishermen and recreational boaters. A major benefit of living along one of the canals is having a boathouse in your backyard, eliminating the need to tow your craft to a public boat ramp.

HOME OF THE DINKY LINE

At the foot of Ollie Avenue, just to the west of the southern entrance to the Fern Canal, is Dinky Dock, a popular place to launch a boat onto Lake Virginia. Currently a public park with a beach open for swimming, it is also an important local historic site. It was the original location of the main railroad station of the Dinky Line, named for the creaking and screeching sounds made by the small, dinky engines of trains that ran from Orlando to Winter Park.

The growth in Central Florida attracted many businessmen, including Walter C. Meloon of Ossipe, New Hampshire, who came to the area in 1924 to seek his fortune during the Florida real estate boom. The following year, he founded the Florida Variety Boat Co., which began manufacturing boats in Pine Castle, just south of Orlando. In 1936, he renamed his company Correct Craft, a name still in use today on a variety of watercraft.

TOURING THE CANALS

In 1937, Meloon announced the establishment of the Venice of America Scenic Pleasure Boat Tours, and the first tour was conducted on January 1, 1938. His twenty-five-passenger boat, *Scenic*, carried a group of businessmen and city officials along the shores of Lakes Virginia, Osceola and Maitland and their connecting canals. Soon, the public was taking the same tour and listening to the pilot's narration of the history of the sites visible from the water.

Now known as the Scenic Boat Tour, it continues as one of the most popular attractions in Winter Park. Six pontoon boats, each carrying eighteen passengers, leave from the dock at the foot of Morse Boulevard and travel about twelve miles over a course that includes sights dating to the town's earliest days. Rollins College, Kraft Azalea Garden, the Albin Polasek Museum & Sculpture Gardens, magnificent homes on the Isle of Sicily and other historic and cultural sites are seen from the water.

One site in particular that can be fully enjoyed only from the water is the Palms, a large home on the east shore of Lake Osceola. Originally the site of a citrus grove bequeathed to Rollins College by Alonzo Rollins, it was sold to carriage accessory manufacturer Edward Hill Brewer after the devastating freezes of 1894 and 1895. Brewer built his large winter cottage there in 1898 with clapboard siding and a wood shingle roof. During the 1920s, the Brewers undertook a major renovation to provide a Georgian Revival façade facing the lake, based on the Brewers' main home in Concord, New York.

The home was later owned by Frederick Detmar Trismen, who sold most of the surrounding land for the construction of additional homes. After

Today's canals and lakes are as popular as ever, and the chain of waterways they form attracts kayakers, canoeists, jet skiers, fishermen and many who prefer to ride in a pontoon boat driven by a knowledgeable tour guide. Here, a group of tourists heads off on a journey into Winter Park's history.

Trismen's death in 1958, the home was acquired by Robert Govern and his family. Seized by the federal government after Govern was convicted of drug trafficking, the house stood vacant for several years. Today it is owned by Mr. and Mrs. Roy Ambinder. The magnificent columned portico can be seen only from the water, either as part of the scenic boat tour or from one of the many boats that cruise the six lakes—Virginia, Mizell, Osceola, Maitland, Nina and Minnehaha—and their connecting canals.

SEE THE SIGHTS

Wildlife is also on display, with Mother Nature putting on quite a show, featuring waterfowl, marine life and even alligators—although not as many as there used to be. An area of Lake Osceola used to be referred to as "Alligator Cove" because so many gators would gather there during mating season in the spring. Eventually, about 150 gators were taken to the Everglades, but some still linger in the lakes and canals.

The waterways offer a living history of Winter Park that one can't see by driving or walking. As one longtime resident put it, "You really have not seen Winter Park until you have gone cruising. In a city of fine homes and beautiful lakes, the residents put their best face to the water."

This article first appeared in the May 2009 issue of Winter Park Magazine. *The first two photos appear courtesy of the Department of College Archives and Special Collections, Olin Library, Rollins College, Winter Park, Florida. The photo of the canal today was taken by the authors.*

Chapter 21

CALLED TO THE
SILVER SCREEN

Chinese Silver Screen Star Made City Her Part-Time Home

In some parts of the country you may see movie and television stars on city streets or in local stores—places such as Los Angeles and New York City. Winter Park can be included on that list, thanks to actresses like Soo Yong, whose face in twentieth-century America was more recognizable than her name.

Soo Yong began life as Ah Hee Young in Wailuku, Hawaii, on the island of Maui. She was the daughter of Young Ming, who arrived in Hawaii in 1875 at age fourteen from China to work on a sugar plantation. His plan was to earn enough money to return to China to find a wife, and three years later he was on his way. But during a stopover in Honolulu, he gambled away all of his money. He began selling dim sum, two for a nickel, and after fifteen years, he had saved enough money to continue his trip to China, where he met Chut Cha. They married and moved to Wailuku.

LIFE IN HAPPY VALLEY

They settled in the taro- and rice-growing region of Happy Valley and raised six children, including Ah Hee, who was born October 31, 1903. All of the children attended Honolulu's Mid-Pacific Institute, a private school. Older sister Harriet was encouraged to continue her studies in Boston, but she couldn't afford that after their father's death. Harriet married Pak Hoy

Wong, a clerk for the Wailuku Sugar Co., and teenage Ah Hee moved in with them to care for their children.

One day, Pak Hoy scolded Ah Hee for having a soda with a Hawaiian boy, which her brother-in-law felt was inappropriate for a Chinese girl. That attitude was common at that time, according to the 2003 book *Chinese Women Pioneers in Hawaii*, a collection of stories assembled by Dorothy Jim Luke and May Lee Chung. One contributor wrote, "It was not uncommon for Chinese men to marry Hawaiian girls, but for a Chinese girl to marry a Hawaiian man was never thought of."

Ah Hee disliked the way she was treated, moved out of her sister's home and wound up in Honolulu. There she earned a living doing household chores and tutoring children of prominent Hawaiian families. She saved her money and used it to attend the University of Hawaii and Columbia University, where she obtained her master's degree in education before becoming a teacher.

CAREER PATH TAKES A JOG

While in school, Ah Hee participated in several theatrical productions, marking the beginning of her interest in acting. She was attending the University of Southern California and working on her doctorate in education when the glitz and glamour of Hollywood shifted her focus from teaching to acting. She had to bluff her way into movie auditions, but her determination paid off. In 1934, she appeared in her first movie, *The Painted Veil*, as a servant to Greta Garbo. She used the name Soo Yong and, thereafter, continued to use that name in the entertainment world and in her personal life.

Soo Yong appeared in more than twenty movies in supporting roles, including as Mae West's maid in *Klondike Annie* (1936); an aunt in 1937's *The Good Earth*, starring Paul Muni; and a telephone operator in *Think Fast, Mr. Moto* (1937). However, supporting roles in those days did not pay the bills, and Asian actresses were not usually offered starring roles. Soo Yong developed a series of monologues about Chinese life that she performed for paying audiences.

As described in *Traditions for Living, Volume II*, a 1989 book published by the Associated Chinese University Women, her monologues "sparkled with wit and satire...These were dramatic and humorous, and she was proud that she had created them herself. Given at universities, clubs and different organizations across the country, Soo captivated her audiences."

One of the many stars with whom Soo Yong appeared was Clark Gable. They are shown here in a scene from 1955's *Soldier of Fortune*.

MARRIED LIFE

Soo Yong met Chun Ku (C.K.) Huang, from Tianjin, China, who was educated at Nankai College and active in the Beijing opera. C.K. opened the Jade Lantern, a seasonal studio business, in Winter Park in the mid-1930s. They married in 1941, and Winter Park became Soo Yong's winter home. She still traveled to Hollywood and international locations to film such movies as *Secret of the Wastelands* (1941), *China* (1943) and *Night Plane from Chungking* (1943). The couple spent summers in Maine, and Soo Yong toured and performed her monologues, but in between, she was at home in Winter Park, working in the store with C.K.

The Jade Lantern was a luxurious Chinese novelty shop on Park Avenue a little north of Central Park. Featured items included Chinese linens, leather goods, arts and crafts, jewelry, picture frames and furniture. A shopper could drop in to buy something and be waited on by a clerk whose face was seen in some of Hollywood's major motion pictures.

FAMILIAR FACE AT ROLLINS

While in Winter Park, Soo Yong became a familiar face at Rollins College. In 1944, she was invited by Hamilton Holt and Edwin Grover to be one of the presenters at their Animated Magazine, and she presented a monologue titled "The Farmer and the Woman." She was one of the most frequent participants at the annual Founders' Week event, also appearing in 1945, 1946, 1948 and 1949.

A month after the February 1946 Animated Magazine, she took part in the student theatrical production of *Lady Precious Stream*, by Chinese playwright S.I. Hsuing. Soo Yong and Donald Allen staged the play, and she designed the costumes and was the first to be seen on stage, as "Honorable Reader." Her husband joined her in the production as one of the two "Property Men" characters, and he also made the cast's hats.

MOVIE CAREER CONTINUES

Soo Yong continued to act in supporting roles in movies including *Peking Express* (1951, starring Joseph Cotton), *Big Jim McLain* (with John Wayne in 1952), *Soldier of Fortune* (1955, with Clark Gable), *Love is a Many Splendored Thing* (1955, with Jennifer Jones), and 1961's *Flower Drum Song*.

In 1961, C.K. and Soo Yong moved from Winter Park to Hawaii. C.K. organized the Honolulu Peking Opera Group, and Soo Yong wrote and performed ethnic improvisational shows. She continued to act but only in productions filmed in Hawaii, appearing in *In Harm's Way* (1965) and James Michener's *The Hawaiians* (1970), which marked the final chapter in her long movie career.

However, she wasn't finished with acting; it was time to move to the small screen. She appeared in four episodes of *Hawaii Five-0*, and C.K. joined her in one episode in 1978, "The Pagoda Factor." He was also in five other episodes without her and usually portrayed a Chinese merchant. Soo Yong completed her television career in 1981 by appearing as a character billed simply as "Old Woman" in a two-part episode of *Magnum P.I.*, titled "Memories are Forever."

After retiring to Hawaii, Soo and C.K. kept in touch with their friends back in Winter Park. This photo taken in Hawaii was part of a Christmas card that they sent to the Congregational church.

"ZEST FOR LIFE"

C.K. died in November 1980, and Soo Yong followed in October 1984. They had no children and willed a large part of their estate to the Chun Ku and Soo Yong Huang Foundation, which they established in 1973 to promote all aspects of Chinese culture in the United States. Soo Yong's niece, Aileen Wong Ho, who wrote about her aunt in *Chinese Women Pioneers in Hawaii* and who was a trustee of the endowment at one time, described her: "She was talented and creative, fun to be with and had a zest for life."

Today, those funds are used for institutional grants and graduate scholarships at the University of Hawaii, promoting Chinese culture, theater and drama. Soo Yong's zest for life continues.

This article first appeared in the August 2010 issue of Winter Park Magazine. *The photo of Soo Yong with Clark Gable appears courtesy of Aileen Ho, Blossom Young Tyau and Lyra Ho Giorgio. The photo of Soo Yong and C.K. Huang appears courtesy of the First Congregational Church of Winter Park.*

Chapter 22

WINTER PARK'S DESTINATION HOTEL

Rich, Well-to-Do Find Home Away from Home at the Langford

Central Florida's reputation as a vacation destination began long before the first theme park was even a dream. Visitors looking to escape the bleak winters of New England and the Midwest found the warm climate irresistible, and many made it their home. In 1934, the same year Robert E. Langford graduated from the University of Chicago, his grandmother visited Winter Park, fell in love with the area and said, "This is the place." She couldn't have known that her choice to buy a nine-year-old house for $12,000 at 716 Interlachen Avenue would lead to her grandson building the prestigious Langford Hotel.

Robert Langford spent a lot of time in Winter Park, and his first major project in the city was the construction of the twenty-four-unit Langford Apartments that opened December 2, 1950, on the north side of New England Avenue, east of Interlachen Avenue. He soon was scouting a location for a first-class hotel somewhere in Florida; his family had owned and operated Chicago's Del Prado Hotel. He considered Fort Lauderdale and a location on the state's west coast, but with a little coaxing from representatives of the city and Rollins College, he decided downtown Winter Park was the best site for a large, modern luxury hotel, which the city hadn't had since the Seminole had burned in 1902.

The grounds of the Langford Hotel reminded one of the major tourist resorts of Miami or other large cities. That was quite a departure from the previous lodgings in quiet Winter Park.

A COOL YEAR-ROUND HOTEL

In addition, he saw the Orlando–Winter Park area as a potential destination for air travelers for business or pleasure. He also recognized the major plus any hotel in hot, sunny Florida would have if it were air-conditioned, an amenity that was missing from local hotels. Earlier hotels in Winter Park were open only for the winter season; a hotel open every day of the year would be different and desirable.

Langford bought land across from his apartments in the early 1950s and made plans, visiting other resorts to see what worked and what didn't. Meanwhile, the city accommodated his needs by rezoning the area from residential to commercial. Langford lived in Chicago with his wife and four children but frequently came to Central Florida while his hotel was in the planning and construction phases. He hired William B. Harvard Jr. of St. Petersburg and B.E. Jolly of Chicago as his architects, and local contractor James Mann Construction Co. was selected to build the hotel.

The *Winter Park Sun* on March 3, 1955, reported that ground would be broken the following week for the million-dollar Langford Hotel. It was scheduled to open on January 1, 1956, an ambitious goal. On January 12, 1956, an editorial in the *Sun* announced that the hotel was about to open:

> *All Winter Park joins this week in congratulating Robert Langford on completion of the Hotel Langford, which will be one of the show places of Winter Park for many years to come.*
>
> *This newspaper would like to give a special word of praise to Mr. Langford for the wide conservation of trees on the hotel grounds, which were saved at great expense. The resultant beauty of the grounds has made the sacrifice well worthwhile. The grapefruit trees around the swimming pool will add tropical interest for the Northern tourist, and the giant oaks make a beautiful background for the tree-top room on the hotel's fifth floor.*

SAVE THE TREES

As part of the Oral Histories project of the Winter Park Library in 1981, Langford recalled his passion about preserving the landscape: "And when I laid out the hotel to save those live oaks that are in the driveway, I took the architect, and I put a string on the area where he could design the building. And I said, 'If you touch those oaks, I'll shoot you in cold blood.' So that's why the hotel's built just where it is."

One of the trees became the centerpiece of the downstairs restaurant known as the Seminole Room, according to Langford's son, Robert "Bob" L. Langford II, named for his grandfather. Bob Langford still lives in Winter Park with his wife, Pam. The eighty-two-room Langford Hotel was located at 300 East New England Avenue and held its grand opening on January 14, 1956, with a dinner-dance in its fifth-floor Tree Top Room, giving attendees an eye-level view of the tops of native slash pines.

HOTEL EXPANDS

In 1957, architect Harvard and the Langford Hotel were presented with an Award of Merit by the Florida Association of Architects. A seven-story addition drew national attention in 1971 when it was announced that the seventy-room expansion would take six days, a seemingly impossible feat. The work in Winter Park did take only six days—if you didn't count nearly two months' work offsite and another month afterward to get the rooms ready for guests.

Robert Langford is pictured here in the early 1960s. Already, he was the best-known hotelier in the city.

The $750,000 addition was built in thirty-two-ton units at a factory in San Antonio, Texas. They were made of reinforced concrete that could be stacked—according to hotel owner Langford and Winter Park architect Ray Bennett—up to forty stories, if one could find a crane tall enough to lift them that high. Guest rooms were manufactured with built-in cabinets, carpeting, wallpaper, bathroom fixtures and dressing tables and were then brought by train to Winter Park. When they reached the hotel, it took only six days to stack them in place.

BIG-TIME TALENT

Another feature of the hotel was big-name entertainment. Musical groups included the Drifters, the Platters and the Shangri-Las. Bob Langford recalled something else that attracted guests: a zoo that was added in the late 1960s. It featured Florida animals, including an alligator, a black bear, a deer, a raccoon and several flamingoes. As the years went by, the population of the zoo increased to more than eighty animals, as local residents donated exotic pets they no longer wanted, including Chinese

This view of a modern air conditioned hotel has been replaced by a condominium on the south side of the lot and empty land on the rest. Perhaps someday plans for building another hotel there will be implemented.

pheasants, an ibis, coatimundi, pot-bellied pigs and woolly monkeys. Laws governing animal habitats changed in later years and would have required costly modifications, so the animals were given to other facilities, including Sea World and Busch Gardens.

In 1978, Langford spent $300,000 to renovate and expand the lobby, introducing Aztec and American Indian motifs, Mexican tile and cedar beams. He took a new direction in 1986 when he spent another $750,000 to give the place the look of a tropical island, and the hotel's "Anchor Room" became the "Bamboo Room."

Even after major Orlando hotels were built and aggressively promoted, the Langford Hotel continued to attract famous clientele that included Walt Disney, Eleanor Roosevelt, Lady Bird Johnson, Ray Charles, Frank Sinatra, Dean Martin, Mamie Eisenhower, John Denver, George McGovern, Bob Dylan, Larry King, Hugh Hefner and Charlton Heston. Ronald and Nancy Reagan picked the Langford for the celebration of their twenty-fifth wedding anniversary in 1977. Later guests included Ron Howard, who checked in wearing his trademark cap to remain low key, and Steve Buscemi, who would wear different disguises but was usually recognized by the attentive staff.

HANDS-ON APPROACH TO SERVICE

That attentiveness paid off for a server in the hotel restaurant during the 1960s. An elderly woman, who spent several months at the hotel each winter, became very ill during one visit. Her compassionate waitress stayed with her that night to care for her. In the morning, the wealthy guest left her a tip of $100,000.

The Langford Hotel was never affiliated with a hotel chain, but the quality of the Langford family's hands-on approach to hotel operation made it popular with European tour operators. The family was well represented at the hotel in the early 1990s, with Langford's daughter, Gerry Liff, as general manager and son, Bob, as vice-president of the company. Langford was named to the Florida Hotel & Motel Association Hall of Fame in 1995. He also received its President's Special Award for a lifetime of distinguished service to the hospitality industry. In addition to his providing Winter Park with a grand hotel, Langford donated land for the construction of the Winter Park Library and the University of Central Florida.

CHECKOUT TIME

The hotel, which had grown to 218 rooms, celebrated its farewell banquet, sponsored by the Winter Park Historical Association, on May 17, 2000, with the theme of "End Of An Era." It gave friends and those who had spent time in the hotel a chance to reminisce about swimming in the seventy-five-foot heated pool surrounded by lush tropical foliage and wildlife; the backlit-in-red grotto bar; the spa resembling a pagoda; the broadcast studio of WLOQ radio; the house band, Jody & the Trouble Brothers; and many more images from the previous forty-four years. A crowd of about two hundred attended the festivities to honor the Langford family. Winter Park mayor Terry Hotard and former mayor Joe Terranova toasted them and the "glorious history of the hotel," according to the Winter Park Library's Archives Collection. The last guests checked out of the hotel on May 30.

Langford was selected by the Winter Park Chamber of Commerce as its Outstanding Citizen of the Year for 2000, and he was honored at its awards luncheon on February 9, 2001. Seven weeks later, he died at the age of eighty-eight. That year, he was one of the first eight inductees into the Florida Tourism Hall of Fame for providing affordable accommodations to Orlando-area visitors during the 1950s with the area's first air-conditioned hotel. The group included Walt Disney and the founders of Carnival Cruise Line, Cypress Gardens, Pan American Airways and the Florida East Coast Railroad.

HOTEL'S FINAL DAYS

The Langford Hotel was sold to a group that had successfully restored several properties in South Beach and was planning to do the same in Winter Park beginning in 2001, but funding dried up after the September 11 terrorist attacks. The hotel was sold to another company and demolished. The Residences at the Regent Winter Park, a seven-story luxury condominium, was later built on part of the land. After plans for two different hotels fell through, Rollins College bought the rest of the land and plans to build a hotel and a small conference center for prospective students and their families, alumni and small scholarly groups. The Langford Hotel is gone, but fond memories remain.

Bob Langford put it simply: "A lot of people ask me if I miss the hotel. I really don't miss the business…but I miss the people."

This article first appeared in the October 2010 issue of Winter Park Magazine. *The photo of Robert Langford appears courtesy of his son, Bob Langford. The images of the hotel are postcards which appear courtesy of Rick Frazee.*

Chapter 23

TOWERING SUCCESS

Mall Offered Shoppers a Chance to Browse Comfortably

C entral Florida was in the midst of a growth spurt in the 1950s, thanks to a booming technological economy. Two large enclosed shopping malls were built to meet the growing population's retail needs. A former T.G. Lee cow pasture south of East Colonial Drive along Bumby Avenue became the home of Colonial Plaza, and about four miles to the north along Orlando Avenue (U.S. Highway 17/92), the Winter Park Mall was built.

SHOP IN AIR-CONDITIONED COMFORT

Shopping malls were a relatively new concept when the Winter Park Mall opened on August 20, 1964. The beautiful, modern mall was considered a symbol of progress, and—with nearly 400,000 square feet of retail space—it also was the largest climate-controlled mall in the Southeast, according to news articles at the time. Anchored by two popular department stores, J.C. Penney Co. on the south and Ivey's on the north, the mall was expected to compete with shops along Park Avenue in downtown Winter Park.

The main entrance on the west side, facing Orlando Avenue, was flanked by two tall white towers that gave the mall a distinctive look. After a trek across a hot parking lot, shoppers were greeted with cool air, lush foliage from numerous large planters suspended from the hallway ceilings and the sound of water falling.

Inside the Winter Park Mall, the "spilling chalice" fountain provided splashing noises and a fine mist that combined with its many plants to provide a comfortable atmosphere for shopping and relaxing.

The mall's centerpiece, located at the junction of the north–south and east–west hallways, was a tall fountain described by some as a "champagne glass" or a tall black "spilling chalice." Water flowed over the edges of the top of the fountain into a stone base, producing a fine mist. When the mall opened, the base of the fountain was encircled by a wooden barrier that also functioned as a low planter. Eventually the barrier was removed and nothing stopped shoppers from walking into the stream of cascading water. Near the fountain was a pet store from which small birds often escaped, giving the mall a tropical ambience with the mist, the rich greenery high and low and wildlife chirping and flying overhead.

In addition to the anchor stores, the mall had a Woolworth's and a Walgreens, each with its own busy luncheonette. Other restaurants came and went over the years, but dining out was not as popular in the 1960s as it is today, and food courts had not yet been developed. The Mall News sold newspapers, magazines, chewing gum and tobacco. Lillie Rubin's was a women's upscale clothing store with well-dressed saleswomen who sold dresses more likely to be seen on Park Avenue than to be worn at McCrory's, a five-and-dime store a few doors down. Children begged their parents to take them to Toy & Hobby Chest.

That's a Really Big Bear!

Community and civic events, as well as fashion shows, were held near the center of the mall. Local businessman Bill Baer sold televisions and other appliances and had a gigantic stuffed bear—not a man-made toy but an actual bear—in his store window that drew crowds of onlookers. Baer's store originated in downtown Orlando. The store was equipped with listening booths, each with two pairs of headsets, to listen to the latest records. As a result, the mall became a place to hang out on a Saturday night with or without a date. One corridor of the mall catered to the artsy crowd and featured paintings and prints for sale.

The Winter Park Mall was well known locally during its first five years, but it had no real national reputation. That all changed Easter morning, April 6, 1969, when it became the first enclosed shopping mall in the United States to have a major fire, according to published reports. Winter Park police were alerted to a problem by a burglar alarm in Lawton's Jewelry that was monitored at the police station. It most likely was triggered by the start of the fire.

Officer Tyler Copeman heard the report on his police radio at 5:04 a.m. while he was patrolling the area and was the first to respond. Once he and another officer were inside, they noticed smoke coming from the roof above the Keller Music store. Suddenly the smoke thickened as the fire spread. The officers radioed for the fire department. By the time the first unit from the Winter Park Fire Rescue Department arrived, the fire was visible outside of the mall. Flames were shooting thirty to forty feet above the roof when firefighters heard a loud hiss, followed by an explosion and the sound of breaking glass.

An Easter Spectacle

The firefighters called for assistance, and two more units from Winter Park, as well as firefighters from Orlando, Killarney and Maitland, responded. As they battled the blaze, a large part of the mall roof collapsed, and it was after 11:00 a.m. before the fire was under control. Thousands of spectators— dressed in everything from pajamas to Easter bonnets—gathered to watch what was, at the time, the costliest fire in metropolitan Orlando's history.

The exact cause of the fire was never determined, but it was thought to have started in either the Singer Sewing Machine Co. or the Taylor-Carlisle Book Store. The state fire marshal ruled out arson, and Winter Park fire chief Robert Blair later said firefighters were hampered by "structural features" that allowed the fire to spread quickly and contributed to the roof's collapse. The only two stores with sprinkler systems at that time were J.C. Penney and Ivey's.

Robert Jacobs, the head of the Winter Park Mall Association, asserted that the mall "met all the code requirements when the mall was built in 1963," but there was little in the code that dealt with enclosed shopping centers. Mallwide sprinkler and fire alarm systems were not included. Blair said, "They sort of had to write the code as it went along," referring to the original construction of the mall. Jacobs assured the public that the association would meet all the amended requirements to prevent another similar disaster.

FIRE SALE

Several stores were able to open the next day—a Monday—and did a booming business. A target date of August 1, 1969, was set for the damaged areas to reopen. Those portions were rebuilt, and the Winter Park Mall was a popular place until the 1980s, when Park Avenue and other area malls appeared to win the battle for shoppers.

By the 1990s, the mall was merely a shell of its former self, with few remaining retailers. Developer Casto Lifestyle Properties suggested the mall be resurrected as a big-box power center, but the city leaders had another vision. They hired consultants Dover, Kohl & Associates to plan a redevelopment as an urban village with offices, shops, restaurants and living space, which would turn the enclosed Winter Park Mall into the rambling Winter Park Village, complete with sidewalks for strolling and parking spaces just a few feet from each store. The final store in the mall closed in the late 1990s, and the Winter Park Village opened a few years later.

MODERN REBIRTH

Nearly all of the Winter Park Mall was demolished. The sole remaining portion, which had been Ivey's and later Dillard's, was redesigned to become the Lofts of Winter Park Village. The fifty-eight rental units feature a curator to manage the art displays upstairs; there is a retail space below that includes the Cheesecake Factory. The village also has several other restaurants, bars and the Regal multiplex cinema, in addition to stores that vary from small, quaint shops to nationally known retailers.

What was once the site of the largest enclosed mall in the Southeast is now enticing visitors and residents to stroll the village streets and enjoy restaurant or sidewalk dining.

This article first appeared in the July 2009 issue of Winter Park Magazine. *The photo of the fountain is from a postcard in the public domain.*

Chapter 24

THAT SINKING FEELING

Hole in Homeowner's Yard Grows Larger Before Her Eyes

In 1939, Mae Rose Williams and her first husband, Fessie, bought five small lots, 125 feet by 100 feet total, at the southwest corner of Denning Drive and Comstock Avenue. They built a three-bedroom house facing north with a good view of the Lake Estates subdivision that had been established in 1925. She had no reason to think that one day her property would attract national attention or that she would have to move out suddenly with no advance notice, thanks to a rapidly developing sinkhole in her front yard.

Mae Rose Williams raised five children after Fessie's death in 1957. She eventually married Tommie Owens and became known as Mae Rose Owens, although the news media often referred to her as Rosa Mae Owens. She was still living in the house during the very dry spring of 1981.

A "SWISH," THEN "PLOOP"

At 8:00 p.m. on Friday, May 8—seventy days after the last rain at the end of February—Mae heard a swishing noise in the front yard. When she looked outside, she saw a sycamore tree disappear as if it were being pulled downward by the roots, making a sound that she described as a "ploop." By early the next day, the hole was close to forty feet wide. In a story in the *Orlando Sentinel*, she said that as the sun rose, she heard a noise "like giant beavers chewing," as the hole began to devour more of her land. The hole was collapsing rapidly.

By noon, as she realized that her home was slipping into the expanding hole, she and the family evacuated and removed their belongings. Within a few hours, the house was irrevocably on its way into the sinkhole's center, headed to unknown depths.

A Growing Concern

To the north, the city swimming pool cracked and emptied, and its deep end fell into the sinkhole. The crater expanded eastward, taking part of the pavement along Denning Drive, and southward to the backs of several businesses that front Fairbanks Avenue, including the Imperial Drive-in Laundry, Action Music, Toppers Color Press and Decorator's Drapery Workroom, damaging a few of the buildings. Several Porsches and a travel trailer awaiting service behind German Car Service, an auto repair shop, fell into the hole. The neighborhood's electric power and telephone service were disrupted.

In this aerial photo taken May 13, 1981, the narrow road coming in from the left is Comstock Avenue, which continued east to intersect with the wider Denning Drive. At the southwest corner of their intersection was the Owens home, which by this time had completely disappeared into the pit.

The spectacle drew many curious onlookers who watched as cars and pieces of buildings disappeared. City planner Jeff Briggs told a *Sentinel* reporter that "it was great photography to see a house swallowed up. And where else do you get Porsches in a sinkhole except Winter Park?" The city erected barriers around the hole and closed part of Fairbanks Avenue until June 29.

SINKHOLE MAKES IT TO THE BIG TIME

The story made the national news, prompting CBS Radio commentator Charles Osgood to recite the following poem: "In Winter Park, Florida, outside Orlando, a troublesome thing can be found; an impressively spacious, expanding, ferocious remarkable hole in the ground."

The national press did not always get it right, however. There were reports that the hole was eight hundred feet across (it was less than half of that), ate part of a six-lane highway (exaggerating the width of Fairbanks), swallowed an entire city block (not quite) and threatened downtown Winter Park and even Orlando.

News of the sinkhole reached Japan, where the manufacturers of the Datsun automobile heard about one of their cars that had gone into the pit with the Porsches and had landed precariously on a ledge. Before it continued downward into oblivion, it was pulled out of the hole with cables. Its owner got into the car, turned the ignition key and drove off. When the executives in Japan heard about that, they contacted the city of Winter Park and asked permission to reenact the incident and film a commercial to show Datsun's reliability. Because of the land's instability at the time, the project was deemed unsafe, and the city turned down the request.

BIRTH OF A SINKHOLE

According to Jim Jammal, a geotechnical engineer based in Winter Park, "It was the largest sinkhole event witnessed by man as a result of natural geological reasons or conditions." He based his statements on his study of two thousand sinkholes over more than forty years. That opinion was echoed by Ardaman & Associates, a local engineering consulting firm. Jammal estimated that the sinkhole had been forming slowly underground for many years and then accelerated its growth about fifty years before Mae Rose Owens saw her sycamore tree disappear.

By the time it finished growing, the sinkhole had consumed about 250,000 cubic yards of soil. From rim to rim, the hole measured 335 feet and reached a depth of 110 feet. It was estimated that it caused $4 million in damages.

Florida has more sinkholes than any other state, and they are relatively common occurrences along the ridge that runs north and south along the middle of the peninsula. Many of the circular lakes found throughout Central Florida are the result of ancient sinkholes—the one in Winter Park drew attention because of its modern formation and its unusually large size.

The porous limestone aquifer under the ground's surface resembles Swiss cheese as a result of the acidic water seeping through and forming small cavities. If the water table falls too low and there is nothing to fill the void, the surface level collapses, and everything above it drops to fill the space like sand in the top of an hourglass.

WHAT NEXT?

It took about a week for the huge hole in Winter Park to stabilize and fill with water. The city then demolished the remains of the city swimming pool, repaired Denning Drive and permanently closed the section of Comstock Avenue west of Denning. The businesses along Fairbanks Avenue were repaired and eventually returned to normal. Twice after the sinkhole stabilized and the base of the hole closed, it unplugged and the water level dropped abruptly to that of the water table. Each time, the "drain" at the bottom replugged, and the lake level retuned to what it is today, with the appearance of a normal lake.

The sinkhole's size and notoriety served as catalysts for the establishment in 1983 of the Florida Sinkhole Institute at the University of Central Florida and for changes in the insurance industry for Florida homeowners.

Workers were able to recover four of the six vehicles that fell into the sinkhole, including the travel trailer, whose owner drove it away, and three of the five Porsches. The other two remain at the bottom of the lake with

This is Lake Rose as it appears today. The photographer was standing approximately at the site of the deep end of the municipal swimming pool, which fell into the sinkhole. But for the huge hole that later filled with water, this view would be of the front of the Owens house.

Mae Rose Owens's home, as well as three other vehicles that were reported by divers in 2009; they saw a Cadillac and a Toyota from the 1980s and a Dodge pickup truck with a 2001 license plate. Apparently, the site that once took expensive cars without their owners' permission had become a place to dispose of unwanted vehicles.

A New Home for Mae Owens

Four months after the sinkhole swallowed her home, Mae and Tommie Owens divorced, and Mae bought a lot at 747 Capen Avenue, where a new home was built for her. In later years, again known as Mae Rose Williams, she lived at the DePugh Nursing Center, just a third of a mile from the sinkhole. She died on September 11, 2005, at age ninety-five, having outlived all of her children. She was buried in Winter Park's Pineywood Cemetery.

The lake that replaced her home was named in her honor. Today, despite its dramatic birth in 1981, Lake Rose is just another of Winter Park's many picturesque areas.

This article first appeared in the May 2010 issue of Winter Park Magazine. *The photo of the sinkhole appears courtesy of Jim Jammal and Nodarse & Associates, Inc. The photo of Lake Rose was taken by the authors.*

BIBLIOGRAPHY

Blackman, William Fremont. *History of Orange County, Florida: Narrative and Biographical.* DeLand, FL: E.O. Painter Printing Co., 1927.

Campen, Richard. *Winter Park Portrait: The Story of Winter Park and Rollins College.* Beachwood, OH: West Summit Press, 1987.

Chapman, Robin. *The Absolutely Essential Guide to Winter Park.* Winter Park, FL: Absolutely Essential Company, 2001.

Douglass, Harry S. *First Congregational Church of Winter Park, Florida, 1884–1984.* Winter Park: Florida Press, 1984.

Jammal, S.E., and Barry F. Beck. *A Self-Guided Field Trip to the Winter Park Sinkhole.* Orlando: Florida Sinkhole Research Institute, 1985.

MacDowell, Claire Leavitt. *Chronological History of Winter Park.* Winter Park, FL: Orange Press, 1950.

Schenck, Noella La Chance. *Winter Park's Old Alabama Hotel.* Winter Park, FL: Anna Publishing, Inc., 1982.

Zheng, Wenxian, David Smith and Patricia Strout. *Walk of Fame: A Rollins Legacy.* Winter Park, FL: Rollins College, 2003.

INDEX

ABOUT THE AUTHORS

G ayle Prince Rajtar was born in Orlando into a family that moved to the city over one hundred years ago. She earned a degree in communications while working as a professional singer and drummer and has remained an Orlando resident. As a freshman at Rollins College in 1971, she met Steve in front of Knowles Memorial Chapel, and they were married there in 1974.

Photo by Billy Goodman.

Steve Rajtar grew up near Cleveland, Ohio; came to Florida for college; earned degrees in mathematics, anthropology, law and taxation; and decided to stay. He has over twenty books published so far, all dealing in some fashion with history, including historical guides for several Central Florida cities.

Since December 2008, they have cowritten the monthly Memories column for *Winter Park Magazine*, and this is their second book collaboration. The first was *A Guide to Historic Winter Park, Florida*, published by The History Press.

Visit us at
www.historypress.net